Python

This book includes:

Python Programming + Python Machine Learning

The Comprehensive Guide to Learn and Apply Python Programming Language Using Best Practices and Advanced Features.

By: Ethem Mining

First book

Python Programming: *A Comprehensive Smart Approach for Total Beginners to Learn Python Language Using Best Practices and Advanced Features.*

Second book

Python Machine Learning: *Understand Python Libraries (Keras, NumPy, Scikit-lear, TensorFlow) for Implementing Machine Learning Models in Order to Build Intelligent Systems.*

Table of Contents

First Book: Python Programming

CHAPTER 5: FUNCTIONS IN PYTHON 123

CHAPTER 6: MODULES IN PYTHON 133

CHAPTER 7: PYTHON DEBUGGING 151

CHAPTER 8: FILES IN PYTHON 165

CONCLUSION 173

Second Book: PYTHON MACHINE LEARNING

Python Programming

A Comprehensive Smart Approach for Total Beginners to Learn Python Language Using Best Practices and Advanced Features

By: Ethem Mining

Introduction

This book is designed to be a step-by-step guide for total beginners to learn to program with Python. This book covers all the basics of Python programming languages from the data object types to debugging methods for large programs. This book has eight chapters where each chapter discusses a specific topic with code examples provided. The present book is structured as follows.

The first chapter of this book provides the big picture of Python programming language, its features as well as its strengths. It also presents the necessary tools in order to start using Python languages and be able to test the examples provided in the book.

The second chapter provides a general idea of what is a variable in Python, how to declare a variable as well as the difference between global and local variables.

Chapter three of this book presents the set of a built-in data object in Python.
It also presents the necessary functions and methods to process these data object type. Chapter four presents first the basics of Python syntax. Although Python is designed as readable with an easy syntax, there are some basic rules to follow which are given in this chapter. This chapter presents the if test and loops syntax and Python exceptions that are used to process data objects that were presented in chapter three.

Chapters five and six discuss how to make your code and scripts more general, reusable, and sharable with other programmers via the notion of functions and modules. Chapter five is dedicated to functions and chapter 6 is dedicated to modules.

Chapter seven of this book is dedicated to debugging with Python. It is common among programmers to use debugging in order to fix any errors in their programs after they are developed. This chapter presents the Python debugger and its commands.

Finally, chapter eight covers processing files with Python. Files are important whether to read from or to write processed data. Writing and reading of the files will also be explained in this chapter.

Plenty of books on this subject are available in the market and we thank you for choosing this one. This book was made with care to make it a useful Python basic book for total beginners that wish to learn to program with Python.

Chapter 1: What You Need to Know Before You Start

The aim of this chapter is to get you started with Python and explain the basics behind Python programming. In fact, this chapter provides you with basics that you need to know before you start learning the basic Python programming language. In this chapter, we discuss what is Python and the Python features that make it an attractive programming language for large domain applications. We also present how you can download and install Python according to your Operating System. We also expose ways on how to launch and execute Python code. Of course, like in any programming language, we will show you how to develop your first famous program 'Hello World'. We won't actually start coding until the next chapters. We expose here just some examples so you can get the general picture behind Python.

What is Python?

Python is a programming language that has several features that makes it very attractive to programmers and developers. First of all, Python is a free programming language which means it is available for anybody. Python is also an open-source language which means you can contribute to the source code if you wish. In fact, Python is a language that is supported by a community that gathers its effort through the internet to improve this language. Python is a language that belongs to the category of high-level languages. This implies that Python does not require compiling like other languages such as C or C++, Fortran, and so on. It implies also that the syntax of Python is very easy to use and learn. These features make Python programs to be easily developed, interpreted, and maintained at low cost. Therefore, it allows sharing and collaborating to develop applications based on Python very efficient.

Being an easy syntax and high-level programming language does not mean that Python is a very slow programming language. In fact, Python is considered a very competitive and productive language. When compared to other programming languages that are low-level and known to be fast, a Python script can be 3rd or 5th size of a similar script developed with C++ or Java. In addition to requiring less typing and debugging, Python does not require compiling. Once a Python script is developed, it can be run directly without additional steps of compiling or linking to other tools or libraries.

Another feature that makes Python an interesting programming language is its portability. Python language is portable and can be run in any Operating environment or system without any changes.

16

The same Python code can be run on Windows, UNIX / LINUX, Mac, on large servers, Android, or iOs tablets. Even graphical user interface applications can be developed to be portable using options that are supported in Python.

Different from other languages like Java or C, Python offers a dynamic typing environment. Variables in Python can be used without declaration or type specification prior to use. Any variable can be used without specifying its type which makes developing codes very straight forward.

A very attractive feature of Python is the libraries that come with it. These libraries, also called packages, are a set of code tools that allows performing basic and common tasks. Python comes with a default library called the standard library which includes a set of modules like the math module for mathematical and numerical programming. Moreover, Python supports using other libraries developed by third parties. There is a wide range of third parties' packages that are available online and allows using advanced tools for

a specific domain (e.g. Numpy library for Numerical programming with Python, Pandas, Matplotlib for developing figures and so on). Hence, when coding with Python language, you have access to a wide set of tools and pre-coded and built-in objects that can be easily used. You never start from scratch because there is a high chance that the function you want to use was already coded and made available for use by anybody.

Python can be considered as a hybrid language in the context that it allows integrating and to be integrated with other programming languages. For instance, you can use pre-coded or compiled libraries that are written in C or C++ within Python. You can also call Python codes from scripts that are written in C or C++.

Overall, If you opt for Python as a language to develop your applications, you get the following benefits: 1) easy syntax and less typing; 2)a program that is fast to execute; 3) a program that is portable and usable within any operating system; 4) a program that is easily maintained and well organized; 5) never start from scratch with access to a wide variety of packages and codes ready to be used; 6) integrated components that allow running codes in C, C++, or any other language to speed up execution of parts of the code. These are some characteristics and benefits of using Python as a language for programming.

What can you develop with Python?

Given the strong features of Python, this programming language can be used to develop a wide range of applications from stand-alone scripts, to graphical user interface applications or integrated programming. In fact, Python is considered as a scripting language to develop easy programs given its readability and easy syntax. However, because it evolved to be also an object-oriented programming language, Python has similar characteristics as the low-level object-oriented languages such as C++. This implies that you can develop modules and classes with Python that benefits from multiple inheritances, polymorphism, and operator overloading. A class is the main notion in object-oriented programming that allows defining an object with its attributes and methods to handle it. So, Python offers the ability to define and develop modular applications.

Python also supports shell script programming that allows developing system programs. Indeed, Python programs are usable on any platform without change, so it is very suitable for shell script programming. These shell scripts are typically used to fetch files, directories, set/change paths, or execute and launch other programs. The POSIX bindings available among the Python standard library support all tools of the Operating system that includes the environment variables, files, filename expansions, command-line arguments, and much more. These tools can be easily handled within Python scripts for shell scripting programming.

Graphical user interface (GUI) applications can be easily developed with Python using the package Tkinter. This library supports graphical user development that is compatible with any operating system, LINUX/UNIX, Mac, and Windows, with no change required.

Python also supports developing internet scripts. A standard Internet module is included in the standard library that comes with Python. This module allows developing scripts that perform networking jobs in the server and in the client. You can develop codes that get information from a server or transfer files via FTP. It allows also processing XML files, and emails (i.e. send, receive or parse).

It allows developing scripts that sort and search internet pages via URL. In addition, you can perform Internet programming where you can develop scripts to generate HTML files and websites. Python can be used as glue programming that launches or runs other programs. For instance, you can easily test libraries written in C or C++ using Python scripts for rapid execution and evaluation.

Python supports numerical and engineering programming, data analysis, and image processing through its libraries Pandas, NumPy, and Matplotlib. Other libraries are available in particular for data analysis.

Python also supports performing database programming. It offers tools to read, save, and perform all common tasks on the database. Moreover, it supports an interface that allows using the traditional syntax of MySQL, Oracle, Sybase, ODBC, or Informix for those who prefer using them.

Those were examples of what you can develop with Python programming language. In general, you can develop anything you want given the panoply of tools and libraries that are available in Python. In addition, Python is a very popular and widely used language in a wide range of applications. Hence, it is always updated and new tools and third parties' libraries are always developed and made available for the public. In addition, Python has a very strong community to help resolve any issues with the language.

Now that you are familiar with Python features and what can you do with Python, let's see how Python can be installed on any Operating System.

How to install Python in your Operating System?

Python is a free programming language that can be downloaded from Python's official website www.Python.org. Python is available as software that includes the standard libraries and the interpreter. The latter is a program in the form of an executable that works, as its name suggests, as an interpreter or translator to the hardware of the machine. Its purpose is to interpret Python codes into a binary form that the machine hardware is able to process. After downloading and installing Python on your machine, several components will be automatically generated that includes the interpreter as executable and the standard library of Python.

If you have Linux or Mac OS, Python might be already available on your operating system. To check if Python is already available, you can type in a prompt shell 'Python'. This should return a '>>>' if Python is available, otherwise, it will display an error message that Python is not recognized as a command line.

Another way to check if Python is available in Linux is to search Python manually in the folders 'usr/local/bin'or '/usr/bin'. If it isn't already available on your LINUX environment, you can download Python for Linux from the Python official website. It comes in several rpm files that can be zipped easily. Python should then be compiled from the source code contained in the zipped directory using the make command and running the config. This should set automatically the configuration of Python in your system. Python generally comes with a README file that explains the instructions to follow in order to install Python.

On Mac OS, Python 2.0 is typically already installed, and basically, you don't have to install or configure anything. However, you can always install the latest version of Python, which is version 3, that is considered the most up to date. Before installing Python, you might need to install OSX-GCC which can be downloaded using Xcode. If you already have Xcode installed, then you don't need to install the GCC. Then you need to install Homebrew.

To do so, you need to launch your OS prompt shell, then execute:

```
$ /usr/bin/ruby -e "$(curl -fsSL
https://raw.githubusercontent.com/Homebrew/install/master/install)"
```

Once Homebrew is installed, you can add it to your path environment variable as follows:

```
export PATH = /usr/local/bin:/usr/local/sbin:$PATH
```

Now, you are ready to install Python using the following command:

```
$ brew install Python
```

If you are using a Windows Operating System, installing Python is very straightforward.
You can download from the Python official website the appropriate version for Windows. The downloaded folder is a zipped directory that comes as a self-installer. You unzip the folder and launch the executable. Then in the installer window, you can click Yes for every window to install Python with the default settings. This should install Python with documentation, graphical user support, an IDLE development as well as the necessary settings you would need to run Python scripts appropriately. After the installation is finished, Python will figure in the start menu among the programs.
Now that you know how to install Python on your machine, we are going to see how you can run Python scripts and, of course, how to make your first program that displays 'Hello World'.

You first 'Hello World' Program

Python can be started from a command line through the prompt of your Operating System. You simply type 'Python' in the prompt. In Windows, for example, this can be done in the WINDOWS DOS console. After running 'Python' command to launch Python interpreter in the prompt, it displays the following 2 Lines:

```
C:\Users\***>Python

Python 3.7.1 (default, Dec 10 2018, 22:54:23) [MSC v.1915 64

bit (AMD64)] :: Anaconda, Inc. on win32

Type "help", "copyright", "credits" or "license" for more
information.
    >>>
```

Basically, it displays the information about the Python version installed and currently launched and commands to get more information. When the prompt displays '>>>', it means that it is ready to execute Python code. To exit Python from the prompt shell on Windows, you can type Ctrl-Z. On Linux or Unix environments, you can use Ctrl-D. Now, we are going to develop and execute your first 'Hello World' program. After you have launched Python in your prompt shell, you can run the following command:

```
>>> print ('Hello World')
Hello World
```

The 'print' command is a function that tells Python to display anything between the parenthesis. We will go through built-in functions in the next chapters. Note here that we are working in an interactive session. Everything that we run is lost once the prompt shell is exited. The code that we type is executed instantly when we hit Enter but lost after ending the session. This is a good way to practice and test quickly some commands. However, it is best suited to save the code somewhere and run it every time you need it. This should save the time of re-writing a script whenever you need it. To do so, you can use a script Editor like Notepad++ to develop and write the script. Then the script should be saved in a file with '.py' extension. This would allow Python to recognize and read the scripts that are written in the file as Python script.

Now, you can write in a text editor the following commands:

```
print ('Hello World')
print ('\n Executing my first Python program')
```

You can save the file as Hello.py. Now, to run this code, you have to launch your operating system prompt shell, then call Python and pass as argument the name of the script we just developed. For instance, on Windows you would type in WINDOWS DOS console:

```
C:\Users\***>Python Hello.py
Hello World
Executing my first Python program
```

24

Note that if in the prompt shell the directory where your Python file is saved is different from your working directory, you should pass as an argument to Python the entire path of your script file like follows:

C:\Users***> Python path_script/Hello.py.

In the second print of this example, we added '\n'; this tells Python to go into the following line.

Chapter 2: Variables in Python

This chapter discusses the Variables in Python. We will start with a definition of what a variable is in Python. Then, we will see how to declare and re-declare variables. We will also see the local and global variables and the difference between these two variables.

What is a variable?

A variable is typically a reserved memory to a saved value on your machine. According to the data type to be stored in a variable, a Python interpreter will allocate memory to save the variable. In Python, variables do not have to be explicitly declared before they are used. In other words, you don't need to define the type or size of any variable before it is used in Python. Basically, Python does not allocate any memory for variables prior to their use. Variables are defined and memory is allocated instantaneously when the variable is used. In Python, variables are objects that can be a number, string, list, dictionary, tuple, or a file. We will explain in detail each data object type in the next chapter. For the sake of simplicity and to explain variables and how to declare and manipulate them in this chapter, we will consider the basic data object number and strings. A number object type can be, for instance, an integer or a decimal.

Before going into how to declare and assign values to variables, there are some rules that should be followed to name a variable or a data object in Python. We cover more of this topic in chapter 4 of this book. First of all, only alpha-numeric characters and underscores can be used to name a Python variable. A variable name cannot start with a numeric. For instance, a variable name can be something like A_20. But 20_A cannot be used as a name for a variable. In Python, variables are case sensitive. For instance, PRICE, price, and Price are three different variables. We will cover more on variable names in Chapter 4 of this book.

How to declare, re-declare, and delete variables?

Remember that in Python, variables do not require any pre-allocation, type, or size specification prior to use. A variable is defined once a value is assigned to it. The equal operator '=' is the operator that assigns values to an object variable. The variable name is the left operand and the value to be stored in the variable is the right operand. For instance, we create the following variable:

>>> A = 200

>>> print (' The variable A is: ', A)

The variable A is: 200

Here we created a number variable.

We can also declare or define several variables in a single statement as follows:

```
>>> A, B, C = 100, 200, 8
>>>print (' The variable A is: ', A)
>>> ('\n The variable B is: ', B)
>>> ('\n The variable C is: ', C)
The variable A is: 100
The variable B is: 200
The variable C is: 8
```

In this example, we declared three number variables in a single statement. We can also declare in a single statement several variables of different types as follows:

```
>>> A, B = 12, 'Price'
>>> print (' The variable A is: ', A)
>>> print ('\n The variable B is: ', B)
The variable A is: 12
The variable B is: Price
```

We can re-declare a variable by assigning a new value to the variable. For example:

```
>>> A = 2000
>>>print (' The variable A is: ', A)
The variable A is: 2000
>>> A = 400
>>>print (' The new value of the variable A is: ', A)
The new value of the variable A is: 400
```

29

We can also change the type of a declared variable by assigning a new type of data. For example, we can declare a variable as a number then we can change its value to a string.

```
>>> A = 100
>>>print (' The variable A is: ', A)
The variable A is: 100
>>> A = 'Date'
>>>print (' The new value of the variable A is: ', A)
The new value of the variable A is: Date
```

Variables in Python can be deleted using the function del. This function is used as followed:

```
>>> A = 100
>>> del A
```

Like assigning multiple variables, the function del can delete multiple variables as follows:

```
>>> A, B, C = 100, 200, 300
>>> del A, B, C
```

Now, if you want to access any variable, Python will throw an error message. For example, if you try displaying variable B:

```
>>> B
Traceback (most recent call last):
File "<stdin>", line 1, in <module>
NameError: name 'B' is not defined
```

Now, you have learned how to declare and re-declare and delete variables in Python. In the next section, we will see what is a local and global variable in Python.

What are the local and global variables?

Remember that in Python, functions and modules can be defined. Variables that are defined inside of these functions are called local variables. Global variables are all variables that are declared in the main script outside of the functions. The global variables can be used inside or outside a function even if they are not defined inside a function. For instance, let's consider the following code:

```
>>> def my_fct():
...         print ('The value of the global variable is:', A)
```

In the code above, we defined a function that displays the value stored in the variable A which is not defined inside the function. So, the variable A is a global variable. Now, we can declare a variable A and print its value by calling the function my_fct() we defined as follows:

```
>>> A = 100
>>> my_fct()
The value of the global variable is: 100
```

Now, let's see how can we change any global variable within a function. For example, we define a function that multiplies the value of the global variable:

```
>>> def my_fct():
...        A = A * 2
...        print (' The value of the variable is: ', A)
```

Now, after we define a variable and call the function my_fct() we defined, we get the following output:

```
>>> A = 1
>>> my_fct()
UnboundLocalError: local variable 'A' referenced before assignment
```

This code throws an error because Python is treating the variable 'A' as a local variable that is not defined inside the function. Therefore, Python cannot recognize it. To be able to change a global variable inside a function, we should use the global keyword. The global keyword is a keyword in Python that enables changing a global variable outside of the current script and makes the changes in a local environment (i.e. inside a function). The global keyword has some rules that should be followed when it is used. The global keyword is used only to read and write (i.e. make changes) to a global variable within a function. Using the global keyword outside of a routine or a function does not have any effect. A global variable defined outside a function is, by default, a global variable and a variable declared inside a function is, by default, a local variable. In the previous example, to change the global variable 'A' inside the function my_fct(), we should add the following command into the function script: global A.

So, the function script should be like follows:

```
>>> def my_fct():
...        global A
...        A = A * 2
...        print (' The value of the variable is: ', A)
```

Now, if you define a variable 'A' outside of the function my_fct() and call the function, we get the following output:

```
>>> A = 1
>>> my_fct()
The value of the variable is: 2
```

Note that the variable is changed also in the script not only inside the function. If we display the variable 'A' outside the function, the value is

```
>>> print (' The value of the variable outside the function is: ', A)
The value of the variable outside the function is: 2
```

If a local variable is declared in a function and then the same variable is declared as a global variable outside a function, calling the function does not change the value of the global variable. To make it more explicit, let's see an example:

```
>>> def f():
...     V = 'Charles'
...     print ('The local variable is:', V)
>>> V = 'John'
>>> f()
The local variable is: Charles
>>> print ('The global variable is:', V)
The local variable is: John
```

Local variables are only accessed within the function. In a script, a local variable cannot be accessed from outside the function where it is defined.

For instance, if we define a function as follows:

```
>>> def f1():
... var = 1
... print (' The local variable is:', var)
```

If we call the function we just defined, the output is as follows:

```
>>> f1()
The local variable is: 1
```

Python throws an error when we try to access the variable 'var' from outside the function as shown below:

```
>>> print(var)
Traceback (most recent call last):
File "<stdin>", line 1, in <module>
NameError: name 'var' is not defined
```

Chapter 3: Python data objects

In this chapter, we will cover the basic data objects in Python. We will also cover the operations that can be performed on these data objects and also how to manipulate them.

What are the Python data objects?

Python data objects are the variables in which save data that will be analyzed or processed. In Python, there are five major data objects types which are: number, strings, lists, dictionaries, and tuples. Numbers are the fundamental data type that also to store numeric variables. Strings in Python are a chain or a sequence of characters. Unlike other languages such as C, in Python, there is no character data object type to save a character singleton. Strings can be a single character or a sequence of characters. Lists are data structure in Python that allows saving items of different types.

In fact, strings are a list that contains only characters. However, lists provide a flexible way to save multiple data of different types in a single data object. Dictionary is another flexible data object that allows in Python to save data of different types in the same data object or variable. The main difference between lists and dictionaries is how the data is stored and how it is fetched. In lists, items are saved from left to right position and are indexed. Items in lists can be accessed using index or position.

On the other hand, items in dictionaries are saved according to a key, meaning that items in dictionaries are not ordered and can be accessed using a key. Items in a dictionary are saved in a randomized way and the only way to access them is by key.

In Python, the function type() allows verifying variables types. This function takes as input a variable and returns the type of the variable passed as input.

Let's some examples of applying this function.

```
>>> A = 200
>>> print ('Type of variable A is: ', type(A))
Type of variable A is: <class 'int'>
>>> A = 'chain of characters'
>>> print ('Type of variable A is: ', type(A))
Type of variable A is: <class 'str'>
>>> A = [1,'p', 300]
>>> print ('Type of variable A is: ', type(A))
Type of variable A is: <class 'list'>
```

In the first example, we defined the variable 'A' as an integer number, the type function returned as output class integer.

In the second example, we declared the variable 'A' as a string, the type function returned a class string. Finally, in the third example, the variable 'A' is declared as a list and the function type returned a class list. Now that you know the different types of data objects in Python, in the next sections of this chapter, we will cover in detail each data type. Let's start with the most basic one, the number data type.

Number Data Object in Python

The number data object is the most basic data object that allows the processing of numeric variables in any programming language. This data object allows the processing quantity data. In Python, a number data object or variable can be an integer, a float number, or a complex number. Python also offers several functions that allow handling this data object. Python also supports normal integer, a long integer with unlimited precision. Basically, integers are a string of decimal digits that can be positive or negative. Float numbers can be a negative or positive number with a decimal point. Python supports the scientific representation of floating numbers with an exponent written with E or e indicating the power. Even though a number with exponent is an integer, Python considers it as a floating number and uses float-point math functions when performing mathematical operations such as addition, subtraction, or multiplication. Python offers all basic mathematical functions and operators to process number variables. The table below summarizes all comparison operators that can be used on number variables. Basically, these operators allow comparing between variables whether they are equal, or if the left operand is superior or inferior to the right operand.

Table 1: Comparison operators to be performed on number variables

Operator	Explanation
X > Y	X is strictly superior to Y
X >= Y	X superior or equal to Y
X < Y	X strictly inferior to Y
X <= Y	X inferior or equal to Y
X == Y	X is equal to Y
X != Y	X is different than Y

In the following table, we cover the logical operators that can be performed on number variables. These operators allow object comparison, whether two variables are true if a number variable belongs to other object data.

Table 2: Logical operators to be performed on number variables.

Operator	Explanation
X and Y	both X and Y should be true (i.e. Y is evaluated unless X is true)
X or Y	X or Y is true (i.e. Y is evaluated unless X is false)
not X	logical negation
X is Y	object comparison
X is not Y	object comparison
X in	X belonging to another object
X not in	X not belonging to another object
|	bitwise or
^	bitwise exclusive
&	bitwise and

The table below summarizes the mathematical operations that Python supports on number variables. These operations include addition, subtraction, multiplication, negation, and division.

Table 3: Mathematical operators to be performed on a number of variables.

Operator	Explanation
X + Y	X plus Y
X - Y	X minus Y
X // Y	X divided by Y
X % Y	The remainder of the division of X by Y
X * Y	X multiplied by Y
+ X	identity of X which equal to X
- X	negation of X
X ** Y	X power Y

Remember that when performing several mathematical operations in one single statement, the rules of mathematical operations applies. That being said, Python will always start by evaluating multiplication first, then it evaluates the other operations. For instance, if we consider the following statement Z = A * X + Y, Python will evaluate A * X then add the result to Y.

If we want to specify a certain order of operations, let's say we want to evaluate first X + Y then multiply the result by A, then we should add parenthesis around X + Y. To do so, the statement should be Z = A * (X + Y). Therefore, the results returned by Z = A * X + Y and Z = A * (X + Y) are very different. When adding parenthesis, Python evaluates first the expressions between parenthesis. Let's apply a real example of the two expressions given above.

>>> A = 4

>>> X = 5

>>> Y = 9

>>> Z = A * X + Y

>>> print ('Z = A * X + Y is:', Z)

Z = A * X + Y is: 29

>>> Z = A * (X + Y)

>>> print ('Z = A * (X + Y) is:', Z)

Z = A * (X + Y) is: 56

We can see from the example above that the first expression Z = A * X +Y returns 29 for A = 4, X = 5 and Y = 9.
Python computes first A * X (i.e. 5 * 4) which is, in this case, 20 and adds Y (i.e. 9) to it which gives 29. For the second expression Z = A * (X + Y), Python evaluates first X + Y (i.e. 5 + 9) which is 14, then it multiplies it by A (i.e. 4) which gives 56. Python supports evaluating multiple expressions in one single line and returns the results in a tuple.

For instance, we can evaluate the two expressions A * X and Z + Y in one single line as follows:

```
>>> A = 4
>>> X = 5
>>> Y = 9
>>> Z = 56
>>> A * X, Z + Y
(20, 65)
```

As we have seen before, we can evaluate the two expressions and assign the results to two variables in one single line.

The code below presents an example:

```
>>> A = 4
>>> X = 5
>>> Y = 9
>>> Z = 56
>>> B, C = A * X, Z + Y
>>> print (' A * X is:', B)
A * X is: 20
>>> print (' Z + Y is:', C)
Z + Y is: 65
```

In the following codes, we provide examples of applying some operators from the tables presented above.

```
>>> A = 4
>>> B = 20
```

Applying division:

```
>>> C= B // A
>>> print (' B divided by A is:', C)
B divided by A is: 5
```

Applying the modulus operator:

```
>>> C = B % A
>>> print (' The remainder of B divided by A is:', C)
The remainder of B divided by A is: 0
```

Operation on integers and float number:

```
>>> A, B = 2.4, 20
>>> C = B // 2.4
>>> print (' B divided by A is:', C)
B divided by A is: 8.0
```

```
>>> print (' The type of the results from an operation applied to
an integer and float is:', type(C))
The type of the results from an operation applied to an integer
and float is: <class 'float'>
```

As we can see from the example above, any operation applied to an integer and a float number always returns a float number type. Python has several built-in mathematical functions available in the math module and comes within the standard library. These functions allow evaluating the trigonometric functions (i.e. cons, sin, tang...), the absolute value of a number, evaluating the integer part of a number, the power function, as well as rounding float number among others. The module math has also the number pi defined.
In order to use these functions, the math module needs to be imported first. In the following codes, we present examples of applying these functions. First, we import the math module:

```
>>> import math
```

Remember, in order to use a function within a module, we need to type module.function_name. For example, for the math module, all functions are called math.function_name. The examples below illustrate how math functions are called.

Using the pi number of the math module:

```
>>> print (' The number pi is:', math.pi)
The number pi is: 3.141592653589793
```

Calling the trigonometric functions from the math module:

```
>>> alpha = math.cos (math.pi)
>>> print (' The cos of pi is:', alpha)
The cos of pi is: -1.0
>>> alpha = math.sin (1)
>>> print (' The sin of 1 is:', alpha)
The sin of 1 is: 0.8414709848078965
>>> alpha = math.tan (1)
>>> print (' The tan of 1 is:', alpha)
The tan of 1 is: 1.5574077246549023
```

Applying the power function is the same as using the operator **:

```
>>> print (' 3 ** 2 is:', C)
3 ** 2 is: 9
>>> C = math.pow (3, 2)
>>> print (' 3 power 2 with pow function is:', C)
3 power 2 with pow function is: 9.0
```

Note that the operator ** returns an integer when the two numbers are integers whereas the math.pow() function always returns a float number. Functions presented in the following examples are from the standard library of Python and not included in the math module.

Evaluating the absolute value of a number:

>>> A, B = abs (-4), abs (6)

>>> print (' The absolute value of -4 and 6 are:', A, 'and', B)

The absolute value of -4 and 6 are: 4 and 6

Evaluating the integer part of a float number:

>>> A = int (6.7)

>>> print ('The integer part of 6.7 is:', A)

The integer part of 6.7 is: 6

Rounding the value of a float number:

>>> A = round (4.5)

>>> print (' The value of rounding 4.5 is:', A)

The value of rounding 4.5 is: 4

String Data Object in Python

Strings in Python are a sequence of characters stored in a list. Unlike other languages like C, for instance, Python does not support a char data object which a character singleton. In Python, a character singleton is basically a string of a single character. Strings in Python are immutable. In other words, once you define a string variable its size is fixed and cannot be changed after. As we mentioned before, a string is a sequence of characters stored in a list which means that string characters are saved in an orderly fashion from left to right. Each character in a string can be accessed by position because it is stored in a list. To declare a variable a string, both single and double quotes can be used. Triple quotes are used when a variable is defined as a block of strings that extends over a few lines. The codes below illustrate examples of declaring variables using single, double and triple quotes.

```
>>> Ex1 = ' This is a string defined in a single quote'
>>> print (Ex1)
This is a string defined in a single quote
>>> Ex2 = " This is a string defined in a double quote"
>>> print (Ex2)
This is a string defined in a double quote
>>> Ex3 = """ This is an example of a string
... that extends on
... three lines """
>>> print (Ex3)
 This is an example of a string
that extends on
three lines
```

In fact, using a single or a double quote does not make any difference. Strings defined using a single or double quote are the same. For instance, we create the same string using both methods, Python will return the same exact result as in the example below:

>>> ' My string ', " My string "

(' My string ', ' My string ')

Python supports several built-in functions that handle strings, unlike other languages. These functions allow concatenation of two strings, repeating the same string, find a sequence of characters in a string, replace a sequence of characters of a string, and splitting a string. The following codes present these functions and illustrate with examples of how they can be used. To concatenate two strings the operator ' + ' can be used. This operator concatenate strings of any length. For instance, we will concatenate the following strings:

>>> A = ' This is the first element of the concatenation example'

>>> B = ' This is the second element of the concatenation

example'

>>> C = ' and this is the third element'

>>> X = A + B + C

>>> print (' The result of concatenation with the operator + is:

\n', X)

The result of concatenation with the operator + is:

This is the first element of the concatenation example This is the second element of the concatenation example and this is the third element

A sequence of a string can be repeated n times using the operator ' * '. For instance:

>>> A = ' This is an example of repeating a sequence of string'

>>> B = A * 2

>>> print (' The string A repeated 2 times is:\n ', B)

The string A repeated 2 times is:

This is an example of repeating a sequence of string This is an example of repeating a sequence of string

To find a character or a sequence of characters within a string, Python has the function find(). This function is a method of the String class object that takes as input a character or a sequence of characters and returns the index of the first character of the sequence in the string.

This method is used as in the example below:

>>> A = ' This is an example of the find function'

>>> A.find ('example ')

11

Remember that a string is a list and items of a string or its characters can be accessed by position. So, for the above example, the position returned by the find function is the position of the first character that was passed as an argument which is in this case ' e '. Therefore, if we try to get the 11th element of the string ' A ' we defined, we get the following output:

>>> A [11]

'e'

A sequence of characters in a string can be replaced using the function replace(). This function is also a method of the String class in Python like the find function and is called in the same manner. The replace function takes two arguments where the first argument is the sequence of characters to be replaced and the second argument is the sequence of characters to be replaced with.

Let's see an example:

>>> A = ' This is an example of using the replace method'

>>> A.replace ('method', 'function')

' This is an example of using the replace function'

In the example above, we replaced ' method ' by ' function ' in the string variable ' A '.

To split a string into several strings, the split function is used. Like the previous methods, the split function is a method of the String class and is used in the same manner. The split function basically split a string according to the spaces in the string. The output is a list of strings where each item is a sequence of characters that forms the strings according to the spaces.

The example below illustrates how this function works:

```
>>> A = ' This is an example of the split function'
>>> C = A. split()
>>> print (' The output of the split function is:\n', C)
The output of the split function is:
['This', 'is', 'an', 'example', 'of', 'the', 'split', 'function']
```

To evaluate the length of a string, the function len is used. This function takes as an argument a variable and it returns its length. In the code below, we illustrate how this function is applied:

```
>>> A = ' This is an example of the len function'
>>> L = len (A)
>>> print ('The length of the string variable A is:', L)
The length of the string variable A is: 38
```

List data object in Python

List data objects are a flexible heterogeneous data object that can contain items of different types. In addition, lists can expand, shrink, and change upon request. A list can be formed by any other data object including lists. Data is typically saved in lists in an orderly manner from left to right. Because items in lists are ordered, they can be accessed by indexing or position. We can perform slicing and indexing and concatenation. Lists in Python are mutable which means their size can be modified after they are defined. This means that we can delete items from a list or add new items to the list by index assignment. Python offers all basic functions to manipulate lists that include concatenation, sorting items in a list, deleting an element from a list, evaluating the length of a list, extending a list, reversing elements of a list, adding an element to a list, or repeating a list n times. The following examples illustrate how to apply these functions and to handle lists in Python.

Lists are defined in Python using brackets. This means that in order to define a list, items to be saved in the list should be written between brackets. For instance:

```
>>> A = [100, 40, 50]
>>> print (' My first list in Python is:', A)
My first list in Python is: [100, 40, 50]
```

Sometimes, it is useful to create an empty list in which we save items as we process information within a loop. We can create an empty list like in the example below:

```
>>> A = []
>>> print (' My first empty list in Python:', A)
My first empty list in Python: []
```

Items of a list can be extracted or accessed by their positions. In Python, indexing starts by 0 meaning that the position of the first element is 0.

For example:

```
>>> A = [100, 40, 50]
>>> print (' The first item in my first list is:', A [0])
The first item in my first list is: 100
```

Python supports slicing to extract or modify items in a list. Note that an item can also be modified by its position. Slicing is typically used when we want to extract multiple elements at the same time.

The examples below illustrate, in more detail, slicing.

```
>>> A = [100, 90, 600, 40, 500]
>>> print (' The first two elements of the list A are:', A [0:2])
The first two elements of the list A are: [100, 90]
>>> print (' The prior to the last element of the list A is:', A [-2])
The prior to the last two elements of the list A is: 40
>>> print (' The last two elements of the list A are:', A [-2:])
The last two elements of the list A are: [40, 500]
>>> print (' The three first elements of the list A are:', A [:3])
The three first elements of the list A are: [100, 90, 600]
```

As you can notice from the examples above, the last index of the slicing is not returned. It only indicates to Python where it should stop the slicing and the actual item corresponding to that index is not returned. The following example is an illustration of the changing values of a list using slicing.

```
>>> A = [100, 90, 600, 40, 500]
>>> A [2:3] = [0,0]
>>> print (' The list after slicing assignment is:', A)
The list after slicing assignment is: [100, 90, 0, 0, 0, 40, 500]
```

When using slicing assignment, the number of new items should be the same as the number of items being replaced. Like in the example above, although we are assigning the same value (i.e. 0), we should assign a list of two items to change the value of the two items.

If we try to assign a single value in this case, Python will throw an error like follows:

```
>>> A [2:3] = 0
Traceback (most recent call last):
 File "<stdin>", line 1, in <module>
TypeError: can only assign an iterable
```

To concatenate two lists, the operator ' + ' is used like for string data object. Concatenation conserves the same order in the lists passed as argument. For example:

```
>>> A = [100, 90, 600, 40, 500]
>>> B = [900, 34, 89, 789, 57]
>>> C = A + B
>>> print (' The concatenated lists is:', C)
The concatenated list is: [100, 90, 600, 40, 500, 900, 34, 89, 789, 57]
```

Like strings, a list can be repeated n times using the operator ' * '.

For example:

```
>>> A = [100, 90, 600, 40, 500]
>>> C = A * 2
>>> print (' My list repeated 2 times is:', C)
My list repeated 2 times is: [100, 90, 600, 40, 500, 100, 90, 600, 40, 500]
```

The length of a list can be evaluated by the basic function of Python the len function. This function returns the number of elements saved in a list.

```
>>> A = [100, 90, 600, 40, 500]
>>> print (' The length of the list A is:', len (A))
The length of the list A is: 5
```

To sort elements of a list, the sort function is used. This function is a method specific to the list class object.
In the example below, we present how this method is used.

```
>>> A = [100, 90, 600, 40, 500]
>>> A.sort()
>>> print (' This is an example of sorting a list and the result is: \n', A)
This is an example of sorting a list and the result is:
[40, 90, 100, 500, 600]
```

The sort function sort items of a list in ascending order. To reverse the items of the list, the method reverse is used. This method is specific to the list class object and is as the sort function.

Now, we can get the list sorted in a descending manner by applying both sorts and reverse like follows:

>>> A = [100, 90, 600, 40, 500]

>>> A.sort()

>>> A.reverse()

>>> print (' The reserved or sorted list A in descending order is:
\n', A)

The reserved or sorted list A in descending order is:

[600, 500, 100, 90, 40]

To add an item to a list, the append function is used. The append function is different than concatenation in the sense that appends is a method specific to list class object and take as input value while concatenation process two lists. They yield the same results in different ways. The append function is useful when you are processing data in a script and updating a list by adding each new item when available.

The append function is called like the sort and reverse methods as follows:

```
>>> A = [100, 90, 600, 40, 500]

>>> A.append(10000)

>>> print (' This is an example of the append function and the
result is: \n', A)

This is an example of the append function and the result is:

[100, 90, 600, 40, 500, 10000]
```

Another function specific to the list class object is extended. This function allows also to add new items to a list. Unlike the append method, extend takes as in input argument a list. The following example illustrates how to add new items with the extend method.

```
>>> A = [100, 90, 600, 40, 500]

>>> A.extend([400, 900, 60])

>>> print ('This is an example of adding items with extend
function: \n', A)

This is an example of adding items with extend function:

[100, 90, 600, 40, 500, 400, 900, 60]
```

In Python two functions allow deleting items from a list which are pop and del functions. The first one, the pop function, deletes and returns the last item of a list. This function is a specific method for the list class object. The second function, the del function, is more general and allows deleting any item or any number of items from a list by position. In the next examples, we illustrate how to use these two functions.

```
>>> A = [100, 90, 600, 40, 500, 400, 900, 60]

>>> A.pop()

60

>>> print (' This is an example of deleting with pop function:

\n', A)

 This is an example of deleting with pop function:

 [100, 90, 600, 40, 500, 400, 900]

>>> del A [2:]

>>> print (' This is an example of deleting items with del function:

\n', A)

 This is an example of deleting items with del function:

 [100, 90]
```

In the example, we deleted all elements from the second item of the list using slicing.

Dictionary data object in Python

The dictionary data object is another flexible data object supported in Python. Dictionaries are heterogeneous data object that enables saving data of different types including another dictionary. Dictionaries and lists both have some similarities in the context that they are both flexible and can shrink and extend upon request.

The main difference between lists and dictionaries is that the way items are saved in these data objects and how they can be fetched. If items in lists are ordered and can be accessed by position, in dictionaries, items are not ordered and are accessed by key. Because dictionaries are a built-in object of Python, they support many data structures that you perhaps can need in developing an application and would have to define manually when working with low-level programming languages. In the same context, they also support several searching algorithms that would need to develop in low-level languages like C for instance. Indeed, using the indexing for dictionaries allows a fast search task. Dictionaries can be used as records or symbols for tables for other languages, or a representation of data structures that are sparse. The main characteristics of dictionaries are as follows. Items of a dictionary are accessed by keys. In fact, items in a dictionary are associated with a key. In other words, a key is assigned for each set of values. When fetching a dataset, keys are used to extract the data that are saved in a particular key.

Indexing operations can also be used to extract items out of a dictionary, however, the index is in the form of a key not a relative position within the dictionary. Items are unordered in a dictionary. Unlike lists, items in a dictionary do not follow a particular order. Python saves items in a dictionary in a random way which allows a fast lookup. The keys that are assigned for each set of data does not provide a physical position but a symbolic position of an item within a dictionary. The length of a dictionary is variable meaning that it can expand or shrink without creating a new copy of the dictionary in question. They are heterogeneous in the sense that they can save in other types of data including lists or another dictionary. Items of a dictionary can be modified in place using index assignment. However, they do not allow the operations in sequences like strings or lists.

Items in dictionaries do not follow any order. Therefore, all operations that are based on a fixed order such as slicing or concatenation are not permitted and do not make any sense when working with dictionaries. However, dictionaries are the single data structure within Python that supports a representation of the category of mapping type meaning that objects can be mapped with keys to values. Finally, dictionaries can be considered as unordered tables. In fact, Python implements dictionaries as hash tables that can start with a small size, then expand if needed. Python uses algorithms that are optimized in order to find keys that make extracting items very fast. Dictionaries in Python are defined by a set of keys for which a set of values are assigned and separated by a comma and enclosed between curly braces. Like lists, Python has several built-in functions that allow handling dictionaries that we are going to cover in the following code examples. The following table summarizes the operations that can be performed on dictionaries.

Table 4: List of operations to be performed on the dictionary data object.

Operator	Explanation
Dic = {}	Declaring an empty dictionary
Dic = {'age':10, 'name': 'john'}	Declaring a dictionary of two items
Dic ['age']	Indexing a dictionary by key
Dic.has_key ('age')	Test of membership
age' in Dic	Test of membership
Dic.keys ()	Get a list of keys
Dic.values ()	Get list of values
Dic.copy ()	Copies items of dictionary
Dic.get (key, default)	Get items
Len (Dic)	Get length of the dictionary
Dic [key] = value	Modifying or adding a value
Del Dic [key]	Deleting items

In the table above, we have an example of defining an empty dictionary and a dictionary of two items. We can also create a dictionary from other dictionaries. To get a sense of how to do so and how to use the functions in the table above, let's practice with some examples in the interactive session of Python.

To create an empty dictionary, we pass empty curly braces:

```
>>> Dic = {}
>>> print (' This is an example of an empty dictionary:', Dic)
This is an example of an empty dictionary: {}
```

To define a dictionary of items, values are assigned to keys. The following codes present an example:

```
>>> Dic = {'Name': 'John', 'Age': 100}
>>> print (' This is an example of an empty dictionary:', Dic)
This is an example of an empty dictionary: {'Name': 'John',
'Age': 100}
```

In the following example, we will see how we can define a dictionary that contains a dictionary.

```
>>> Dic = {' Pers': {' Name': 'John', 'Age': 10}}
>>> print (' This is an example of nested dictionary:', Dic)
This is an example of nested dictionary: {'Pers': {'Name': 'John',
'Age': 10}}
```

A dictionary can be also defined from lists. In the previous examples, each key is associated with single values. In the following examples, we illustrate how we can define a dictionary where each key is associated with a list of values.

```
>>> LL = ['John', 'Mike', 'Dave']

>>> Ag = [20, 30, 40]

>>> Dic = {'Name': LL, 'Age': Ag}

>>> print (' This is an example of a dictionary defined from
lists:', dic)
   This is an example of a dictionary defined from lists: {'Name':
   ['John', 'Mike', 'Dave'], 'Age': [20, 30, 40]}
```

To extract items from a dictionary, we use the same syntax of position indexing used for lists. The difference is we use keys instead of position.
Let's see some real examples of how to extract items from a dictionary.

```
>>> LL = ['John', 'Mike', 'Dave']

>>> Ag = [20, 30, 40]

>>> dic = {'Name': LL, 'Age': Ag}

>>> print (' This is an example of extracting an item from a
dictionary: \n', dic ['Name'])
   This is an example of extracting an item from a dictionary:
   ['John', 'Mike', 'Dave']
```

To extract keys of a dictionary, the keys method is used as follows:

```
>>> LL = ['John', 'Mike', 'Dave']
>>> Ag = [20, 30, 40]
>>> dic = {'Name': LL, 'Age': Ag}
>>> print (' This is an example of extracting keys of dictionary,
keys are: \n', dic.keys())
This is an example of extracting keys of dictionary, keys are:
dict_keys (['Name', 'Age'])
```

We can verify if a key is part of a dictionary by using the logical in. The following presents an illustration of verifying the existence of a key in a dictionary.

```
>>> LL = ['John', 'Mike', 'Dave']
>>> Ag = [20, 30, 40]
>>> dic = {'Name': LL, 'Age': Ag}
>>> print ('This is an example of verifying if a key (here Age) is
in dictionary:', 'Age' in dic)
This is an example of verifying if a key (here Age) is in
dictionary: True
```

The len function is a general function in Python that returns the length of a data object. It is applied to the dictionary the same as it is applied to lists and strings.

```
>>> LL = ['John', 'Mike', 'Dave']
>>> Ag = [20, 30, 40]
>>> dic = {'Name': LL, 'Age': Ag}
>>> print (' The length of the dictionary is:', len (dic ))
The length of the dictionary is: 2
```

Values stored in a dictionary are extracted using the method values. This function is used as follows:

```
>>> LL = ['John', 'Mike', 'Dave']
>>> Ag = [20, 30, 40]
>>> dic = {'Name': LL, 'Age': Ag}
>>> print (' This is an example of extracting values of a
dictionary:\n', dic.values ())
This is an example of extracting values of a dictionary:
 dict_values ([['John', 'Mike', 'Dave'], [20, 30, 40]])
```

Values stored in a dictionary can be replaced in place without creating a new dictionary. To do so, position indexing by key is used. The following code presents an example of changing values by key.

```
>>> LL = ['John', 'Mike', 'Dave']
>>> Ag = [20, 30, 40]
>>> dic = {'Name': LL, 'Age': Ag}
>>> print (' Dictionary before replacement:', dic)
Dictionary before replacement: {'Name': ['John', 'Mike', 'Dave'],
'Age': [20, 30, 40]}
>>> dic ['Name'] = ['Markus', 'David', 'Peter']
>>> print (' Dictionary after replacement:', dic)
Dictionary after replacement: {'Name': ['Markus', 'David',
'Peter'], 'Age': [20, 30, 40]}
```

Items from a dictionary can be deleted using position indexing and the del function.

For instance

```
>>> LL = ['John', 'Mike', 'Dave']
>>> Ag = [20, 30, 40]
>>> dic = {'Name': LL, 'Age': Ag}
>>> print (' Dictionary before deletion is:', dic)
Dictionary before deletion is: {'Name': ['Markus', 'David', 'Peter'],
'Age': [20, 30, 40]}
>>> del dic ['Age']
>>> print (' Dictionary after deletion is:', dic)
Dictionary after deletion is: {'Name': ['Markus', 'David', 'Peter']}
```

Items can be added to a dictionary using position indexing like in the following example:

```
>>> LL = ['John', 'Mike', 'Dave']
>>> dic = {'Name': LL}
>>> print (' Dictionary before adding new item is:', dic)
Dictionary before adding new item is: {'Name': ['Markus', 'David',
'Peter']}
>>> dic ['Age'] = [90, 30, 50]
>>> print (' Dictionary after adding new item is:', dic)
Dictionary after adding new item is: {'Name': ['Markus', 'David',
'Peter'], 'Age': [90, 30, 50]}
```

So far, we covered in this chapter all basic and flexible data objects supported by Python. In the next section, we will cover the last data object which is tuples. This data object is relatively simple to handle, and as you can see, you already learned basics functions that might be used on tuples too from reading these sections about the other data objects.

Tuples data object in Python

Tuples like dictionaries and lists are a collection of data of different types. Tuples are very similar to lists. However, tuples cannot be changed. Indeed, tuples are less flexible than lists and are immutable. Items of tuples are typically written between parenthesis instead of brackets like lists. Tuples have similar characteristics as lists. Items in tuples are ordered according to their positions. Items in a tuple can be accessed by their positions. Therefore, tuples support indexing, slicing, concatenation, repetition, and globally all operations performed on strings and lists. Tuples are similar to string in the context that both do not allow changing in size or items in place. Tuples cannot expand or shrink and their size is fixed once it is defined. The heterogeneous data object supports storing data of different types. In the following code examples, we illustrate how to perform some operations like indexing, concatenation, slicing, and others on tuples.

First, we illustrate some examples of defining a tuple.

```
>>> A = ()
>>> print (' This is an example of an empty tuple: ', A)
This is an example of an empty tuple: ()
>>> A = (1,)
>>> print (' This is an example of a one item tuple: ', A)
This is an example of a one item tuple: (1,)
>>> A = (1, 'John', 6.7, 90)
>>> print (' This is an example of a 4 items tuple: ', A)
This is an example of a 4 items tuple: (1, 'John', 6.7, 90)
>>> A = 1, 'John', 6.7, 90
>>> print (' This is another example of a 4 items tuple same as
the one before: \n', A)
This is another example of a 4 items tuple same as the one
before:
 (1, 'John', 6.7, 90)
>>> A = 1, 'John', (6.7, 90)
>>> print (' This is an example of a nested tuple: ', A)
This is an example of a nested tuple: (1, 'John', (6.7, 90))
```

Note from the examples above that if values assigned to a variable without brackets or parenthesis, Python will automatically consider the variable as a tuple.

Although in the case of tuples, parenthesis is optional. In order to declare a variable as a tuple, it is a best practice to use parenthesis. This also helps code readability. Note also that parenthesis in Python encloses an expression. So, if a tuple from a single item is to be declared, use the syntax presented in the examples above. If a single value is written between parenthesis, it will not consider it as tuple but rather just a value. Tuples have no specific methods like lists. However, the basic Python operations performed on lists and strings apply to tuples as well.

To concatenate two tuples, the operator ' +' is used. For example:

```
>>> A = (1, 4, 60)
>>> B = (90, 50, 40)
>>> print (' This is an example of tuple concatenation: ', A + B)
This is an example of tuple concatenation: (1, 4, 60, 90, 50, 40)
```

To repeat a tuple n times, the operator ' *' is used as in the example below:

```
>>> A = (1, 4, 60)
>>> print (' This is an example of tuple repeated 2 times: ', A * 2)
This is an example of tuple repeated 2 times: (1, 4, 60, 1, 4, 60)
```

To extract an item from a tuple, we can use either indexing or slicing as illustrated in the examples below:

>>> A = (1, 4, 60)

>>> print (' This is an example of extracting an item from a tuple by indexing: ', A [1])

This is an example of extracting an item from a tuple by

indexing: 4

>>> print ('This is an example of extracting an item from a tuple by slicing: ', A [:1])

This is an example of extracting an item from a tuple by slicing:

(1,)

Note that when extracting items from a tuple, it returns a tuple even though it is a single value. To sort items stored in a tuple, it should be converted to a list then sorted. Like mentioned before, tuples do not have specific methods like lists. The following example illustrates how to order a tuple:

>>> A = (100, 4, 60)

>>> print (' This is a tuple before sorting: ', A)

This is a tuple before sorting: (100, 4, 60)

>>> T = list (A)

>>> print (' This is a tuple converted to a list: ', list(A))

This is a tuple converted to a list: [100, 4, 60]

>>> T.sort ()

>>> print (' This is the list sorted', T)

This is the list sorted [4, 60, 100]

>>> A = tuple (T)

>>> print (' This is the tuple sorted: ', A)

This is the tuple sorted: (4, 60, 100)

Note that the function list() allows converting an item to a list and the tuple() function convert an object to a tuple. In fact, both functions list() and tuple() create new objects. Here, we just have overwritten the existing ones which makes it like a conversion of data types. The immutability characteristics apply only to the tuple data object and not to items that it contains. For instance, if a tuple contains a list, the size of the list can be changed but not the tuple itself. Let's see an example to make it more comprehensible.

>>> A = (' Name', [20, 40, 50], 0)

>>> print (' This is an example of a tuple containing a list:', A)

This is an example of a tuple containing a list: ('Name', [20, 40, 50], 0)

>>> A [1][2] = 9000

>>> print ('This is an example of changing an item in a list within a tuple:', A)

This is an example of changing an item in a list within a tuple: ('Name', [20, 40, 9000], 0)

If we try to change an item from the tuple like follows, Python throws an error:

```
>>> A [1] = 'Age'
Traceback (most recent call last):
 File "<stdin>", line 1, in <module>
TypeError: 'tuple' object does not support item assignment
```

In this chapter, we covered all built-in data objects in Python which are number, strings, lists, dictionaries, and tuples. The last data object, tuples, are heterogeneous data object that allows storing data of different type like lists and dictionaries but is less flexible. You are probably wondering why to use tuples. If they are not flexible, using lists instead would make more sense. Indeed, lists are more flexible, but they can be changed through your script. On the contrary, tuples cannot be changed or altered after they are defined. In addition, tuples may be of interest where lists cannot, for instance, as keys for dictionaries. Also, some functions in Python require variable in the form of tuples, not lists. As a general rule, lists are the go-to when the data need to be in ordered data structure and may be changed throughout the script. Otherwise, tuples are the best choice.

Chapter 4: Python Operators

In this chapter, we will cover the different statements in Python as well as the Boolean expressions and conditional statement which are the if tests and loops. Overall, we will cover the statements that allow processing data that are stored in the data object that we presented in the previous chapter. At the end of this chapter, you will acquire basic skills to develop and run some logic Python scripts.

Python Statements Syntax

Before diving into logic if test and loops and logic conditions, we are going to run over the basic syntax of Python. Statements are basically the expression you write that instruct what the Python interpreter should do. In other words, statements are instructions into your program. In the following table, we present a global statement that can be used in Python.

Table 5: List of Statements supported in Python.

Statement	Explanation	Illustration
Assignment	Create a variable	A, B = 90, 'Age'
		print (' This is an
print	Display objects	example')
call	Launching a function	stdout.write('Example\n'

		)
		while T: print
while else	Global loop	('Example')
	Iteration in a	
for else	sequence	for i in list: print(i)
		if A in text: print
if/elif/else	Selection of tasks	('Example if test')
break and	To jump into a	
continue	specific task in loops	while T: if not A: break
try, except		try: tasks / except: print
and finally	Exceptions catching	('Example Error')
	To trigger an	
raise	exception	raise Endlocation
import	Module importing	import math
	Import from a	
import from	module	from sys import stdout
def, return		
and yield	Defining functions	def fct(a): return a * 3
		class subclass:
class	To build objects	newData=[]
	Defining a global	def fct(): global a,
global	variable	return a * 3
del	To delete items	del data
assert	To check to debug	assert A == B

Statements that are related to larger programming subjects like developing functions, modules, and debugging will be covered separately in the upcoming chapters of this book. Chapters are dedicated to each programming subject. In this chapter, we will cover the assignment syntax, expression statements, the if test, and the loops. Let's start with the basic statement which is the assignment.

So far, in this chapter, we have been already using the assignment statement. The assignment statement allows assigning a data object to a variable name. Basically, you write an assignment statement using the operator '=' where on the left, you have the target, and the on the right is that the data to be assigned. The target can be either a variable name or component of an object. On the right can be a single value or an expression that evaluates an object. Overall, the assignment is very simple, but you should consider some properties. Assignment in Python saves objects references in names or data structure. When an assignment is used, it does not copy the object, but it creates a reference to the object.

Unlike C language, for example, variables in Python are similar to pointers and not just data storage. This means when you use or modify a variable inside a function, it is modified through the entire script not just locally. On the contrary, if a variable in C is modified in a function, it is modified only locally and not in the whole script. When first assigned, names are created. In Python, a variable name is created on the first time you assign a value to it. Python does not require a pre-declaration of variable names beforehand.

When assigned, the variable name is replaced by the value that references in each expression they belong to. Before being referenced, the variable name must be assigned.

If a variable name is used before it is assigned to a reference data object, Python throws an error. Python uses some other implicit assignments when importing modules, defining functions or classes, in function arguments that we will see later in this book. Assignment works the same in any context and whether it is implicit or explicit, the assignment always binds an object reference to a variable name. Assignment has a few forms that are presented in the table below.

Table 6: Forms of Assignment Statements

Statement	Explanation
A = 5	Basic assignment form
A, B = 5, 6	Multiple assignment
A = 5, 6	Assignment of tuple
A = (5, 6)	Assignment of tuple
A = [4, 5]	Assignment of list
A = B = 'true'	Multiple target assignment

The first two forms of the assignment are the most basic forms. The three following forms of assignment (list and tuple assignment) are called list /tuple unpacking assignment. In these forms of assignment, Python creates first a tuple /list of the elements on the right. Then it pairs from left to right to the variable name.

The last form assignment, multiple target assignment, Python assigns the same data reference to multiple target variables. This assignment is the same as writing two lines of codes to assign A = 'true' and B = 'true'. In the following code examples, we will cover some illustration of assignment forms and tricks coding in Python.

Here we present some basic unpacking assignments.

```
>>> Age = 30
>>> Name = ' John'
>>> A, B = Age, Name
>>> print (' This is an example of tuple unpacking assignment: ')
>>> A, B
(30, ' John')
>>> [X, Y] = [Age, Name]
>>> print (' This is an example of list unpacking assignment: ', X, Y)
This is an example of list unpacking assignment: [30, ' John']
```

The reference values found on the right is stored in a temporary tuple. Since the temporary tuple is defined by Python, tuple unpacking assignment may be used to replace 2 variables while not having to define a temporary variable.

The following example illustrates how to swap two variables with unpacking assignment.


```
>>> Age = 30
>>> Name = 'John'
>>> Age, Name
(30, 'John')
>>> Name, Age = Age, Name
>>> print ('This is an example of swapping variables with
unpacking assignment: ')
This is an example of swapping variables with unpacking
assignment:
>>> Age, Name
('John', 30)
```


In Python, any sequence of values or data can be assigned to a tuple or list on the condition that the sequence has the same length. A list of values can be assigned to a tuple and vice-versa. A string can also be assigned to a tuple. In general, Python would assign the right items to the left items in sequence from left to right by position.

Let's see some illustrations.

```
>>> [X, Y, Z] = (30, 400, 50)
>>> print (' This is an example of assigning a tuple to a list:')
This is an example of assigning a tuple to a list:
>>> X, Y, Z
(30, 400, 50)
>>> (X, Y, Z) = 'ade'
>>> print (' This is an example of assigning a string to a tuple:')
This is an example of assigning a string to a tuple:
>>> X, Y, Z
('a', 'd', 'e')
```

An unpacking assignment allows assigning a sequence of integer to multiple variables. In fact, Python has a built-in function which is a range that returns a sequence of integers. This function is very useful when working with for loops that we are going to see later in this chapter. In the next example, we provide an illustration of assigning a series of integers to a tuple.

```
>>> A, B, C = range (3)
>>> print (' This is an example assigning a sequence of integers:',
A, B, C)
This is an example assigning a sequence of integers: 0 1 2
```

Now that we have covered the assignment statement, it is worth mentioning that rules should be respected when choosing a variable name. We have already seen in Chapter 2 of this book that variable names should always start by an underscore or a letter and only alpha-numeric characters are permitted. In general, a name of a variable should respect the following syntax: letter or underscore + letter, underscore or digit. A named variable like 1_var, var# or $%var is not permitted variable names. In Python, the case is important and variables names are case sensitive. For instance, Var, var, and VAR are three different variable names. Python has reversed words that are permitted to be variable names. Basically, these reversed words are lowercase and are used by the Python system.

For instance, if you try assigning a value to 'and ' Python will throw a syntax error:

```
>>> and = 4

File "<stdin>", line 1

and = 4

^

SyntaxError: invalid syntax
```

The same variable name can be used if it is uppercase:

```
>>> AND = 4

>>> AND

4
```

Overall, the reversed words cannot be redefined. This applies also to module and function names. You might be able to define a module as ' and.py' or a function as ' and() ', but Python will generate an error when you try to call the function or import the module.

The following table presents all reversed words that are not permitted as variable names.

Table 7: Reverse word in Python not permitted as variable names.

and	elif	global	or	yield
assert	else	if	pass	def
break	except	import	print	continue
class	exec	del	from	for
finally	in	is	return	try
lambda	while	not	raise	

In addition to the rules mentioned above to name a variable, there are some conventions that should be considered. They are a requirement but considered the common practice. The names of the variables that end and start with 2 underscores, for example, __X__, are typically considered by the interpreter of Python as system variable names. Naming variables in that manner should be avoided. The statement ' from module import ' cannot import names with a single underscore like _name.

If a variable name starts with two underscores and does not end with another two, it is located to enclosing classes. A name that is only in the form of a single underscore (i.e. _) save the last expression result in the interactive session of Python. These were the major naming rules and conventions that you should consider when choosing a name to a variable. In the following examples, we are going to cover some useful assignment statement that is commonly used within the if test and loops that we are going to cover later in this chapter. These assignment statements are inspired by the C programming language and mainly a shorthand. They typically combine an assignment with a binary expression. The following table summarizes these statements known as augmented assignment statements.

Table 8: List of Python augmented assignment.

Assignment	Equivalent	Assignment	Equivalent
A += B	A = A + B	A -= B	A = A - B
A &= B	A = A & B	A ** = Y	A = A ** B
A // = B	A = A // B	A /= B	A = A / B
A %= B	A = A % B	A | = B	A = A | B

Let's go back to the Python interactive session and see some examples of these assignments. We start first by the operator '+='.

```
>>> A = 10
>>> A = A + 1
>>> print (' A incremented by traditional assignment:', A)
A incremented by traditional assignment: 11
>>> A = 10
>>> A += 1
>>> print (' A incremented by augmented assignment:', A)
A incremented by augmented assignment: 11
```

Note that both yield to the very same results. However, the augmented assignment ' A += 1 ' is faster because Python needs to evaluate the variable 'A' one time. On the contrary with the basic form ' A = A + 1', the variable needs to be evaluated twice because it appears in the expression twice. This augmented assignment '+=' works as concatenation when applied to strings and, as mentioned, works faster than the basic concatenation formulation.

```
>>> A = 'Example'
>>> A += ' number 1'
>>> print (' This is an example of augmented assignment
on strings type:', A)
This is an example of augmented assignment on strings
type: Example number 1
```

The same augmented assignment can be applied to a list. For instance,

```
>>> List = [30, 40, 50]
>>> List += [2, 5, 8]
>>> print (' This is an example of augmented assignment
on List type:', List)
This is an example of augmented assignment on List type:
[30, 40, 50, 2, 5, 8]
```

In short, augmented assignment perform faster because variables on the left need to be evaluated once and require less typing. In addition, they allow the interpreter to choose automatically the best technique to evaluate the expression. If an object supports in-place modification like lists, the augmented assignment would perform the in-place modification instead of creating a copy.

Syntax rules in Python

Before diving into if test and loops, in this section, we are going to address the syntax rules that should be followed when coding with Python. Python syntax is generally simple. However, there are some rules to respect. Globally, there are no braces or parentheses around the statements block in Python. Instead, Python relies on indentation to delimit or group blocks of code nested under a header.

Unlike other programming languages, Python does not use a semicolon to indicate the end of the statement. The line end is the statement end on that particular line. When launched, program statements are executed by Python from first to last until there is an indication to jump a block of statements. Python would jump a block of statements if it meets an if a test or a loop as we are going to see later in this chapter. These statements are called the control flow because they control which statements to run or to jump. Blank lines are generally ignored by the interpreter as well as lines starting by a ' # ' character.

In fact, any line that starts with the ' # ' character is considered a comment. Hence, it is ignored by the Python interpreter.

There is another type of comments supported by Python that is known as the documentation strings. They are also known as docstrings in short. This form of comment is retained by the Python interpreter. They show up at the header of a program file. They are associated with objects and can also be printed alongside the documentation. Although Python interpreter retains the docstrings, they are ignored.

Remember that indentation is very important in Python and indicates the level of a block. If the indentation is not used appropriately and consistently, Python throws an error. The if statements and loops generally have a header line as we are going to see in the following chapters. Block of codes to run each header whether it is a loop or an if test.

Globally, when developing a Python program, the form or syntax of the program should look like:

Code block level 0

Header statement:

    Code block level 1

    Header statement:

        Code block level 2

        ....

    Code block level 1

Code block level 0

Note that in the example syntax presented above, each code block line up to the right in the same distance as considered from the same block. Codes that are deeply nested are just more intended to the right compared to the upper enclosing code. If a statement doesn't fit in a single line because it is too long, there are few rules to respect to make them continue on a few lines. Python support continuing a statement in more than one line if it is enclosed between brackets, parenthesis, or curly braces. All statements that are between parenthesis, assigning lists, dictionaries, and tuples can be performed on more than one line. These statements end at the line where the closing part appears.

Only the first line where the statement begins should be intended correctly and the continuous lines can be at any level. For instance, we declare in the following example a list on several lines:

```
>>> A = [ 9,
... 8,
... 10,
... 100]
>>> print (' That was a list declaration on multiple lines:', A)
That was a list declaration on multiple lines: [9, 8, 10, 100]
```

This type of statements continuing on several lines can be used for anything between () like expressions, or function headers or arguments.

For example:

```
>>> A = 2
>>> B = 3
>>> if (A == 1
... and B == 3):
... print ('YES')
... else:
... print('NO')
...
NO
```

Note that in this example, only the statement under the header of the if and else statements should be intended. The continuing line of the if the header does not have to be intended.

Python support writing more than one statement in one line separated by a semicolon. For instance:

```
>>> A = 3; B = 90; C = 900
>>> print (' That was an example of multiple statements in a single line:', A, B, C)
That was an example of multiple statements in a single line: 3 90 900
```

Python If Test and Its Variations

This chapter section will cover the if test which is a statement that allows choosing from a series of possible operations according to the result of a test. In this, we will cover also the Boolean expressions and truth tests. We will also see in detail the embedded statement syntax. The if statement is typically a formal procedure in programming languages. This statement is in the form of if test then a set of options of operations to perform or another elif (i.e. else if) and ends with a block of else. The block of else is optional. After every test (if and elif) and else, there is an embedded block of operations that is indented under the test header. When running Python on if test, it performs the block of operations that are assigned to the first test which is satisfied (i.e. returns true) otherwise, it performs the else block if all tests are not true.

Basically, the if statement takes the general form presented below:

```
if < condition or test >:
        < block of statements >
elif < condition or test >:
        < block of statements >
else:
        < block of statements >
```

Only the if statement and the associated block are required. The other elif and else blocks are optional.
Let's practice some examples in the interactive session and see how the if statement how works under Python.
In the very basic case, an if statement can be run alone when you need to run an operation when a condition is met.

The following code example provides an illustration.

```
>>> X = 9
>>> if (X == 9):
... print (' YES ')
...
YES
```

Notice here that the prompt changed to ' ... ' which means the continuation of lines in the basic Operating system. If working in IDLE, you have to intend the block after the If header. Here in the interactive session, a blank line ends the statement and runs the if block. In the following code, we illustrate the most common form used of the if test:

```
>>> X = 0
>>> if (X == 9):
... print (' YES ')
... else:
... print (' NO ')
...
NO
```

In the next code example, we provide an illustration of the complete form of the if statement with all blocks. This is typically used when you have multiple conditions to evaluate in order to choose to right operations to perform within your code.

```
>>> A = ' TIGER '
>>> if (A == 'John '):
... print ('HOW are you, John?')
... elif (A == 'Dog'):
... print (' What is the name of the dog? ')
... else:
... print (' WARNING: DANGER ')
...
WARNING: DANGER
```

Note that, in this example, Python runs through all blocks because they all return false statement. Now, you might be wondering how to select an action based on the value of a variable. In fact, Python does not have a switch or case statements like C programming language or Pascal. f you are not familiar with these programming languages, the switch and case are statements that allow performing an action according to its value. In Python, the if/elif/else statement is used in series instead.

In the following example, we provide an illustration of performing an operation based on the value of the variable ' A '.

```
>>> A = 3
>>> if (A == 1):
... print (' The month is January')
... elif (A == 2):
... print (' The month is February')
... elif (A == 3):
... print (' The month is March')
... else:
... print (' This is another month')
...
The month is March
```

Another way to implement this example and requires less typing is by using a dictionary. In fact, a dictionary associates with each key value. To use a dictionary in the previous example, we should do something like:

```
>>> B = {'1': ' The month is January ', ' 2 ': ' The month is
February ',
...       '3': ' The month is March '}
>>> print (B.get (' 1 '))
This month is January
>>> print (B.get (5))
None
```

Note here that when a key is not found in the dictionary, it returns None by default which would be like the else statement in an if test. In short, dictionaries can be a very good alternative to implement a simple procedure that selects an option according to variable possible values where these possible values are the keys of the dictionary. In the rest of this section, we are going to discuss the truth test that is usually used within an if test. In the previous chapters, we have introduced comparisons operator used on strings and numbers and so on. Basically, these are Boolean operators that return True or False, 0 or 1 depending on the operation or the comparison used. Overall, true is returned when an object is a non-zero number or not empty. False is returned if an object is zero number or empty or is None. The equality test and comparisons are applied to data objects and return 1 or 0.

The logic operators 'and' and 'or' returns true or false. Let's see some examples in the Python interactive session.

```
>>> A = 3
>>> B = 5
>>> A == 3 and B == 4
False
>>> A == 3 or B == 4
True
>>> [] or 5
5
```

Note here that in the last line, Python evaluates both the left and the right side and returns the right value or because the left is false. Basically, when used in an if test or a while loop, Python uses a Boolean which is a logical true or false.

Loops in Python (while and for loop)

In this section, we discuss the main two loops in Python that repeats a block of code over and over. The first loop format is the while loop which supports a general looping statement and the second loop format is the for loop that goes through elements of a sequence data structure and runs a specific code. Other forms of loops are supported in Python that includes 'break' and 'continue' which we will cover in the next section. A while loop is a broad form of iteration construct. The while loop typically runs the same code over and over as long as a condition is true.

When this is evaluated to false, Python interpreter skips the code intended under the while header and runs the following code statements.

In the simplest form of the while loop, the syntax is as follows:

```
while < test or condition >:
        Block of code
```

Python will run, in this case, the block of code until the test is evaluated to false. The other form of Python is more complex looks like:

```
while < test or condition >:
        Block of code
else:
        Block of code 2
```

In this form, Python will run the block of code 2 if it does not exit the while loop with a break.

Now, let's go back to the interactive session of Python and see some examples of a while loop.

```
>>> A = ' NAME '
>>> while A:
... print (' This is an example of while loop:', A)
... A = A [1:]
...
This is an example of while loop: NAME
This is an example of while loop: AME
This is an example of while loop: ME
This is an example of while loop: E
```

In this example, the while loop runs the code as long as the variable 'A ' is not empty. The code consists of printing the value of the variable 'A' and removing one character. Note that one major problem that you should pay attention to when using the while loop is that this loop may run forever if the test is always evaluated as true. Hence, checking and making sure that the test is evaluated to false at some point to exit the loop. The for loop consist of iterating through elements of a sequence object that can be string, list, dictionary, tuple or any other class object. Basically, the number of iterations is known beforehand unlike the while loop that runs according to a test value.

The for loop syntax is very easy and takes the form of a header line and block of statements to run over and over and optionally an else statement like the while loop. The header of the for loop indicates a target and the data object that it iterates trough. The general syntax is as follows:

```
for < i > in < data object >:
        block of code
else:
        block of code 2
```

When running a for loop, Python attribute elements of the data object to the 'i' variable. Then it evaluates the block of the code for each item of the data object stored in 'i'.

This variable 'i' is assigned in the header of the loop and can be changed inside the loop and is updated automatically to the next element in the sequence whenever the control is evaluating the header of the loop. Typically, this variable takes the value of the last item evaluated in the sequence when the loop is over. If the loop did not exit with a break statement and was run accurately, the variable 'i' would refer to the very last item in the sequence. The optional else block works similarly as for the while loop. If the for loop did not exit with a break, it will run the code block assigned to the else statement. Now, let's see examples in the interactive session of Python. The first example presents an illustration of applying a for loop on a list of strings. This example goes through string items of a list and prints each element.

```
>>> List = ['John', 'Brian', 'Mike', 'James']
>>> for i in List:
... print ('Name is:', i)
...
Name is: John
Name is: Brian
Name is: Mike
Name is: James
```

Note here that in the loop, each string element is assigned to the variable 'i'. We can also use the position indexing to loop over items of a list. For the previous example, we would do:

```
>>> List = ['John', 'Brian', 'Mike', 'James']
>>> for i in range (len (List)):
... print ('Name is:', List [i])
...
Name is: John
Name is: Brian
Name is: Mike
Name is: James
```

The second application of the for loop is useful when you are assigning elements from the sequence to another sequence by position. We will see in the next example an application of the for loop on a list of numbers.

In this example, we compute the sum of elements of a list.

```
>>> A = [10, 200, 4, -100]
>>> X = 0
>>> for i in A:
... X+= i
... print (' A loop example on list of numbers, the sum is:', X)
...
A loop example on list of numbers, the sum is: 10
A loop example on list of numbers, the sum is: 210
A loop example on list of numbers, the sum is: 214
A loop example on list of numbers, the sum is: 114
```

If a single statement is to be evaluated within the loop body, the for loop header and the statement can be written in the same line. For instance, the previous example becomes without the print statement as:

```
>>> A = [10, 200, 4, -100]
>>> X = 0
>>> for i in A: X+=i
...
>>> print (' This is an example of for loop in a single statement, the sum is:', X)
This is an example of for loop in a single statement, the sum is: 114
```

The for loop works the same on a sequence of tuples where the target value will be assigned a tuple.

The following two examples illustrate how the for loop work on a tuple sequence.

```
>>> T = ('John', 'Mike', ' Samuel')
>>> for i in T:
... print ('Name in the tuple is:', i)
...
Name in the tuple is: John
Name in the tuple is: Mike
Name in the tuple is: Samuel
```

If a list of tuples is provided the loop for works the same.

For instance:

```
>>> T = [ ('John', 30), ('Mike', 40), ('Samuel', 40)]
>>> for i in T:
... print ('Name and age in list of tuples is:', i)
...
Name and age in list of tuples is: ('John', 30)
Name and age in list of tuples is: ('Mike', 40)
Name and age in list of tuples is: ('Samuel', 40)
```

In the above example, at each iteration, the target variable ' i ' is assigned a tuple that is in the list sequence.
Another way to use the loop for, in this case, is to iterate through two-variable targets where each variable is assigned an element of the tuple in the list.

We can apply this to the previous example as follows:

```
>>> T = [ ('John', 30), ('Mike', 40), ('Samuel', 40)]
>>> for (i, j) in T:
... print (' Name in the list tuple is', i, 'Age in the list tuple is', j)
...
Name in the list tuple is John Age in the list tuple is 30
Name in the list tuple is Mike Age in the list tuple is 40
Name in the list tuple is Samuel Age in the list tuple is 40
```

A function that is useful when working with loops, in particular, the for loop is the range function. This function basically takes as an input of one or two arguments. Then it generates a sequence of order values according to the value of the input arguments. If only one argument is supplied as input, then it generates values in the range 0 to the input value. If it is supplied with two input arguments, then it generates values from the first input value to the second input value.

The following code presents an illustration of the range function supplied with one and two arguments.

```
>>> for i in range (4):
... print ('Example of range with one input argument here 4, values are:', i)
...
Example of range with one input argument here 4, values are: 0
Example of range with one input argument here 4, values are: 1
Example of range with one input argument here 4, values are: 2
Example of range with one input argument here 4, values are: 3
>>> for i in range (3, 6):
... print ('Example of range with 2 input arguments here 3 & 6, values are:',
i)
...
Example of range with 2 input arguments here 3 & 6, values are: 3
Example of range with 2 input arguments here 3 & 6, values are: 4
Example of range with 2 input arguments here 3 & 6, values are: 5
```

We can pass optionally the third argument to the range function. When supplied, this argument is used as a step to generate values from the first to the second input argument values.

The next example provides an illustration of the range function supplied with three input arguments.

```
>>> for i in range (3, 10, 2):
... print ('Example of range with 3 input arguments here 3 & 10 & 2, values
are:', i)
...
Example of range with 3 input arguments here 3 & 10 & 2, values are: 3
Example of range with 3 input arguments here 3 & 10 & 2, values are: 5
Example of range with 3 input arguments here 3 & 10 & 2, values are: 7
Example of range with 3 input arguments here 3 & 10 & 2, values are: 9
```

Notice that whether it is supplied by one or two input arguments, the range function does not include this input value in the returned range values. As you can see from these examples, the range function is very useful with loops to repeat a sequence of operations over and over for a specific number of times.

The while loop and the for loop can have a much-complicated syntax that allows jumping or exiting the loop when a specific condition is met or a test that evaluates to true. In general, loops can be associated with the statement's break and continue. In the next section, we cover the usage of break and continue within loops of Python.

Continue, Break and Pass Statements with Python Loops

Now that you have seen Python loops, while and for, we will cover the two statements continue and break. These statements only work within a loop. We will also see in more detail the else statement which is related to the break statement. The break statement allows jumping all the codes enclosed in the closest loop. In other words, it exits the enclosing loop. The continue statement, on the other hand, jumps to the closest enclosing loop header. The pass statement is equivalent to not doing anything which is basically a placeholder of an empty statement. The pass statement is typically used when there is no required action to take and works as an empty body for a statement that is compounded.

Given these definitions, the general complex format of the while loop is as follows:

```
while < test or condition >:
        Block of code
        if <test 1 or condition 1>: break
        if <test or condition 2>: continue

else:
        Block of code 2
```

Note that the break and continue can be placed anywhere within the body loop. However, they are typically placed within an if test to operate as a response to the returned value of a test or a condition as presented above. Now, let's go back to an interactive session to see some examples.

In this first example, we will see how the continue statement allows jumping nested statements.

The illustration presented displays all odd numbers inferior to 10 and jumps even numbers.

```
>>> A = 10
>>> while A:
... A = A - 1
... if ((A % 2) == 0): continue
... print(A)
...
9
7
5
3
1
```

In this example, there is no need to enclose the print statement within an if test because the continue statement will skip it if the test ' (A % 2) == 0 ' is evaluated to true.

Hence, the print statement is run only if the continue statement is not run. The continue statement used here is similar to a 'goto' in other programming languages. If you are just starting with Python, it is best to use continue sparingly.

The above example can be written in a more readable way with the print statement assigned to an if test as follows:

```
>>> A = 10
>>> while A:
... A = A - 1
... if (A % 2 != 0) :
... print(A)
...
9
7
5
3
1
```

The next example provides an illustration of the while loop with a break statement.

In this example, we read input data from the user until he writes an end.

```
>>> name= []
>>> while name != 'end':
...        name = input ('Enter a name, to stop enter end: ')
Enter a name, to stop enter end: 'John'
Enter a name, to stop enter end: 'Mike'
Enter a name, to stop enter end: 'Liam'
Enter a name, to stop enter end: 4
Enter a name, to stop enter end: end
>>>
```

The function input() here is a function of Python version 3 that reads input from the keyboard. Note that when the loop keeps reading from the standard input until the end is entered. Then Python returned >>> into the prompt which means it is ready to take other statements. In the following example, we illustrate how to combine the break and the else statements in a while loop. In this example, we determine if a given number is prime or not by looking for the numbers factors which are superior to 1.

```
>>> A = 7
>>> B = A / 2
>>> while B > 1:
... if (B % A == 0):
... print (A, ' is factor of', B)
... break
... B = B - 1
... else:
... print (' The number', B, 'is prime')
...
The number 0.5 is prime
```

The break here is very useful that works as a flag when exiting the while loop.

In this example, instead of adding an if test to evaluate the value after the while loop is over, a break is inserted to exit when a factor is found. Otherwise, if the break is not met, the loop assumes that a number is a prime number. Note that even if the loop does not run at all in case the header is false, to begin with, it will return or run the statement assigned to the else because it did not exit with a break in this case. If we try that on the previous example (i.e. B == 0), we still get the message 'The number is prime'.

```
>>> B = 0
>>> while B > 1:
... if (B % A == 0):
... print (A, ' is factor of', B)
... break
... B = B - 1
... else:
... print (' The number', B, 'is prime')
...
The number 0 is prime
```

The else might seem a bit confusing because it is specific to Python's programming. You can think of the else as a way of coding some flags that catch the exit of a loop without explicitly hard coding test to check those flags. Let's say that you are coding a loop that search for an item in a sequence of values and you want to know, after the loop is over, whether it was found or not.

You might think of coding something that looks like the following code:

```
>>>A = [20, 200, 2, 90]
>>>inList = 'NO'
>>>i = 0
>>> while (i < len (A) and inList == 'NO'):
...         if (A [i] == 0):
...                     inList = 'YES'
...         else:
...                     i = i+1
>>>if (inList == 'NO'):
...         print ('Is not in list ')
... else:
...         print ('Is in list')
Is not in list
```

Here, we have set a flag 'inlist' initialized as 'NO' that we check after the loop is executed to know if the item is in a list or not. This structure of code is what the break and the else statement are designed for. By implementing these two statements, the above code is optimized. First, the loop is stopped once the item is found in the list by inserting the break statement. Second, the else code will be displayed if the loop is run over all items and not found the item. In addition, we have fewer intermediate variables to handle.

The optimized code with break and else statement is as follows:

```
>>> A = [20, 200, 2, 90]
>>> i = 0
>>> while (i < len (A)):
...         if (A [i] == 0): break
...         i = i+1
... else:
...         print ('Is not in the list')
Is not in the list
```

In the same manner, the for loop uses the else and break statements to exit the for loop when a condition is satisfied. The complex form of the for loop is as follows:

```
for < i > in < data object >:
        block of code
        if < condition 1 or test 1 >:
                block of code 2
                break
        if < condition 2 or test 2 >:
                block of code 2
                continue
    else:
        block of code 3
```

Like the while loop, when test 1 is evaluated to true, the for loop is exited and the else block is not run. When test 2 is evaluated to true, every statement that appears after is ignored and the loop goes to the header (i.e. evaluate the next item). Now that you understand the sophisticated format of the for loop, let's see some examples in an interactive session.

The following example is similar to the last example of the while loop. We search for an item in a list. This example illustrates also how to use nested loops. We use the break and else statement to exit and return if the item is on the list.

```
>>> A = [20, 40, 90, 50, 60]
>>> B = [9, 90, 'no', 90, 20, 100]
>>>for j in B:
...        for i in A:
...                if j == i:
...                        print ('Element', j, 'is in list')
...                        break
...        else:
...                print ('Element', j, 'is not in list')
Element 20 is in list Element
100 is not in list Element
90 is in list Element
100 is not in list Element
100 is not in list
```

In this example, the first loop goes through the first list 'B's that stores the items being searched for and the second loop goes through the list that is being searched. Both loops are running together. When an item is found in list 'A', the second loop is exited. The else here is assigned to the second loop to return that the item is not the list. The code presented here is just to present an illustration of using a break and else. This code can be optimized by using the 'in' operator that looks for any match in a sequence. The optimized code is as follows:

```
>>> A = [20, 40, 90, 50, 60]
>>> B = [9, 90, 'no', 90, 20, 100]
>>> for j in B:
...     if j in A:
            print ('Element', j, 'is in list')
...     else:
...             print ('Element', j, 'is not in list')
Element 9 is not in list
Element 90 is in list
Element no is not in list
Element 90 is in list
Element 20 is in list
Element 100 is not in list
```

This code only works for the lists defined here. It would be helpful to be able to run the same code on other lists, too. This is when the function comes very handy. We will cover this topic in the next chapter.

The loops we have covered in this section will also be used in chapter 8 of this book that covers files. Indeed, loops are very handy to repeat the same task as long as it is necessary. Files come in the form of several lines that contains several characters. They are the typical use of the for loops. In chapter 8, we will cover how to use loops to read and write files.

Python Exceptions

Python exceptions are events that can have an impact or change the control flow of a script. Exceptions in Python are raised on errors. They can be raised and intercepted by the script. In Python, exceptions are handled using three statements that we will cover in this section.

The first statement try has two variations which are ' try/ finally ' and ' try/ except'. The first variation, 'try/ except', catches the exceptions and recovers from it by Python or by the user. The second variation, ' try/finally ', performs a clean-up whether the exception is raised or not. The second statement is ' raise ' and it triggers an exception in the code manually. The third statement is ' assert'. This statement raises an exception conditionally in the script. Now you must be wondering why to use exceptions in a script.

Exceptions are very handy in large programs to keep track if the code is running as expected. In other words, exceptions allow jumping pieces of code when something goes wrong.

Depending on what is expected from the program, when an exception is raised, the code might execute some tasks to recover from the exception that was raised or exit the code completely. In Python, exceptions are used for a wide range of purposes. Exceptions can be used to handle errors. Python is able to automatically trigger errors when it is running. These errors can be caught and assigned a code/task as a response or can be ignored. If the error is being ignored, Python would use the default handling of the error. The program will stop running and an error message will be displayed. Otherwise, if you develop a try statement as a response when the error is being raised, Python would ignore the default handling and would jump to your coded try statement. Hence, your script will continue running after the try. Exceptions can also be used as a notification for events. In this context, exceptions are used as a validation condition signal without handling and coding flags that are processed in the program. For example, a routine that searches for a particular element might trigger an exception when failed instead of returning a Boolean or integer, as a result, to be tested after.

Exceptions can serve to handle a special case. A special case is a condition that can occur rarely. Instead of convoluting the code to take action, an exception can be inserted to take action when unusual cases occur. Exceptions can be used to stop actions. As mentioned before, the ' try/finally ' statement guarantees that code final closing tasks are executed whether an exception is raised or not during run time. Finally, the exceptions can be used as flow control similar to a ' goto ' statement available in other programming languages. Now that you got the general idea behind exceptions, let's try some examples in the interactive session.

Try/except statement

The syntax for this exception statement is in the following form:

```
try:
 statement or task to run
except < name >:
 statement
```

In order to illustrate the ' try/except ' statement, let's consider a function that we will run as a task in the try block. We define a function that takes as input two arguments where the first is a list and the second is an index. This function returns the element of the index passed as a second argument. Don't worry about functions at this step. We will cover them in more detail in the next chapter.

```
>>>def fct (myList, ind):
...      return (myList[ind])
```

Now, if we try to call this function with the list and the index defined below, we get something like:

```
>>> myList = [20, 40, 50, 70]

>>> ind = 3

>>> A = fct (myList, ind)

>>> print (' element is: ', A)

element is: 70
```

Now, if we try to pass an index equal to superior to 3, Python will throw an error as follows:

```
>>> ind = 8
>>> A = fct (myList, ind)
Traceback (most recent call last):
File "<stdin>", line 1, in <module>
File "<stdin>", line 2, in fct
IndexError: list index out of range
```

Python detects automatically that the index passed is out of the range of the list indices.

Then, it raises an error handled by the default IndexError exception which prints a message error along with the number of the lines where the error occurred. Here we are working in an interactive session, so the lines are not meaningful. If real applications where the program is not run in the interactive session, the program will be stopped from execution by the default top handler. Python throws this error because it is not being raised by the defined function.

You can also try to catch the exception when running the function and not trigger the default Python hander using the ' try/except ' statement.
The code will be, in this case, to run the function as follows:

```
>>> try:
...         fct (myList, 9)
... except IndexError:
...         print (' This is an exception')
...
This is an exception
>>>
```

In this case, Python ignores the default handler and jumps to the defined handler. The try has stopped the function from running. Then Python displays >>> in the prompt which means it is ready to run statement. In more complex programs and real applications, to recover and catch from the exceptions, you can use the try statement. Then, we would define something like:

```
>>> def catcher():
...         try:
...                 fct (myList, 9)
...         except IndexError:
...         print (' This is an exceptions')
... print (' Will continue running')
...
>>> catcher()
This is an exception
Will continue running
>>>
```

Now, the exception is being raised by try, and the program continued running after the exception by printing the message ' Will continue running'. The program resumes normally and runs the following statements.

Try /finally statement

In this sub-section, we illustrate how the ' try/finally ' works. The ' try/finally ' syntax is similar to the ' try/exception ' syntax and is in the form presented below:

```
try:
 statement or task to run
finally:
 statement or task to run
```

This exception statement runs the code assigned to finally, whether try raised an exception or not.

```
>>> Mylist = [20, 300, 900, 90]
>>> ind = 2
>>> try:
...      fct (Mylist, ind)
... finally:
...      print (' This is the finally block')
...
900
This is the finally block
```

Here the finally block is launched with the try block that runs normally without any exception being raised and the script continued running after the try block. This code is similar to displaying the message in the finally block after running the function. So, the code is similar to the following statements:

```
>>> ind = 2

>>> myList = [20, 300, 900, 90]

>>> fct(myList, ind)
900
>>> print ('This is the finally block')
This is the finally block
```

However, in a real application where the code is run outside of the interactive session if the function triggers an exception every code statement after it is not executed. So, we might try a code that resumes after the try statement if something went wrong.

For example

```
>>> def after():
...    try:
...        fct (myList, 9)
...    finally:
...        print ('This is the finally block')
...    print ('This the block after try and finally')
...
>>> after()
This is the finally block
Traceback (most recent call last):
  File "<stdin>", line 1, in <module>
  File "<stdin>", line 3, in after
  File "<stdin>", line 2, in fct
IndexError: list index out of range
```

Now, you can notice the code did not display the message 'This the block after try and finally'. The reason is that the control flow does not continue when an exception is triggered in the try/finally statement. Python executes the code assigned to finally. Then it propagates the error raised in the try section through the code to the default handler in this case. If the function call is changed for a case where it does not raise an error, the code after the try/finally would run. The code below shows an example:

```
>>> def after():
...        try:
...        fct(myList,0)
...        finally:
...        print ('This the finally block')
...        print ('This the block after try and finally')
...
>>> after()
This the finally block
This the block after try and finally
```

Chapter 5: Functions in Python

This chapter of the book covers functions that are a piece of code that can be executed repeatedly with different variables to generate a different outcome. We have been already using this notion in the previous chapters whether it is using Python's built-in function like print() to display a message in standard output of Python or the function that we defined in the section illustrating exceptions. This chapter makes the emphasis on how to develop functions that compute and return values and how to code a script to be reused easily.

Function Utilities in Programming

Functions are a fundamental concept in any programming language. They are also known as procedures or routines in other programming languages. Functions are very handy when you need to run the same code with different variable values. For instance, you want to compute the factorial of different numbers. Instead of coding the same code for each number, you would define a function that takes as input the number of interests, computes its factorial, and returns the result. This way you just have to call the same function for each number inside a loop for instance.

In this context, functions serve for two main purposes. The first is to make the code reusable. They provide a way to package your code such that it is used more than once or in multiple places in the same or different program.

So far, illustrations and code examples presented in this book are run immediately in the interactive session. With functions, the code can be wrapped and generalized to be used several times after. The second purpose of functions is to decompose a program into several pieces where each piece is assigned a role. This is very useful when coding a large program or a framework that replicates the functioning of a complex system. Functions allow us to break down the system into pieces where each piece is coded by a function. Each function would serve to perform a task in a large system. This way of coding makes it easy to implement complex systems than just implementing a whole system in one chunk of code. You can think of functions as a procedure that allows replicating how to do something. Coding functions does not imply different syntax. In the following sections, we will cover the keywords and the basics to develop functions with Python.

Function Concept, Declaration and Calling in Python

We have been using and calling functions that are built-in Python in the earlier chapters of this book. For example, to compute the length of an object, we call the function len. In this section, we are going to learn how to define new functions. Every new function you define in Python works exactly the same as the built-in functions of Python. Functions are called through statements or expressions and can take input arguments and return a result. Developing new functions requires using additional statements that were presented in table 5 shown in Chapter 4.

In Python, functions act differently compared to complied programming languages (e.g. C or C++).

'def ', a new statement, defines the Python functions. This is also an executable code. When you develop a new function, it is not recognized by the Python until it hits a 'def ' statement and runs through it. Sometimes, the 'def ' statement is inserted in if test or a loop or maybe inside other 'def ' statement. In a real application, the 'def ' statements are defined within modules. When the module is imported in the Python environment workspace, the functions are generated automatically. We will cover modules in more detail in the next chapter. The 'def ' statement makes a new object (i.e. a function) and assigns a name to it. A function object is created and given a name every time a 'def ' statement is found by Python. This name is the reference of the function which can be saved in a list or given another name. Functions can send back an object result after they are called. When Python goes through a statement that calls a function, it runs through the function code until it finishes. Then it resumes to the following statements. If a function returns a value, it communicates it back to the control flow as a return statement. This result is then the outcome of calling this function. Functions can take optionally input arguments that passed as a reference.

Unlike other programming languages such as C or C++, references (i.e. variables) are shared across the function and Python called. This means that a variable that is modified within a function is also modified automatically within the entire code. In other words, if you define a variable name outside a function.

Then, later in the code, you call a function that shares the same variable name (i.e. reference) that changes its values.

When the function is finished running and the control is given back to the controller, the variable has the same value that was assigned inside the function and not the value that was assigned before the function call.

As we have mentioned in Chapter 2, variables that are assigned inside a function are, by default, local variables. They are defined only inside the function. Once the function finishes running, these variables don't exist anymore. Like any other object data, the function does not need any declaration of any kind prior to use. Inputs arguments, as well as output arguments, can be of any type of data object. Hence, the functions can be called with different data types.

To create a new function, we use the 'def ' statement with the following syntax:

```
def < function name> (argument 1, ...., argument n):

    statements or tasks to perform
```

Like any compound statement in Python, indentation is very imported. All statements that constitute the function body should be intended unless it is one single statement that can appear after the header (i.e. after the colon). The function body is executed every time the function is called. After 'def ' is the name of the function which attributed to reference to the function object, followed by the arguments. The name of arguments is attributed to the data object that is passed to the function when called.

If no argument is to be passed to the function, then the syntax is as follows:

```
def < function name> ():
        statements or tasks to perform
```

Usually, a function returns an output argument or statement. In this case, the syntax of the function includes a return statement as follow:

```
def < function name> (argument 1, ...., argument n):
        statements or tasks to perform
        return < output value>
```

In Python, the 'def ' can appear anywhere in the code, even inside other statement. For example, we can define a function according to a test like follows:

```
If < condition >:
        def my_function():
                statement 1
else:
        def my_function(argument):
                statement 2
```

In the syntax example given above, the function my_function is defined with or without input argument depending on whether the condition is satisfied or not. The 'def ' statement works as any Python assignment statement and the function is not defined until the code goes through the 'def ' statement. The function name can also be changed anytime by assigning it to another name. For instance, we can do:

Name2= my_function

To call a function we just type in the name of the function with arguments if it takes any.

function_name (argument 1, argument 2, ..., argument 3)

Or   function_name ()

In the following sections of this chapter, we are going to present explicitly how functions use arguments and return values with some examples.

Function Expressions, Arguments, and Returned outputs

As we have seen in the previous section, arguments of a function, also called parameters, are passed between parenthesis. When the function is called, Python uses these arguments to reference the date object passed as input. There is no requirement to declare the type of the data object that the function is expecting as input. Usually, functions are defined within modules and run outside of the interactive session. For the sake of simplicity and the fact we are using simple basic examples, the interactive prompt would be sufficient to run the examples of this book.

The following code is an example of a function that takes as an argument a number, computes and displays a factorial of a number.

```
>>> def Xfactorial (X):
...     P = 1
...     for i in range (1, X + 1):
...         P *= i
...     print ('Factorial of ', X, 'is:', P)
```

Now, to call this function, we simply type the name of the function with the number for which we want to compute the factorial.

For example:

```
>>> Xfactorial (3)
Factorial of 3 is: 6
```

If we want to save the output of this function in a later use in the code, we use the return statement when defining the function as follows:

```
>>> def Xfactorial (X):
...      P = 1
...      for i in range (1, X + 1):
...            P *= i
...      return P
```

Then when calling the function, we assign the function to a variable as follows:

```
>>> A = Xfactorial (3)
>>> print ('Factorial 3 is:', A)
Factorial 3 is: 6
```

Now, let's consider a simple function that returns the value of X times Y with X and Y two input arguments.

```
>>> def Prod (A, B):
...      return A * B
```

Now, let's call this function with input arguments of different types.

>>> A = Prod (2, 3)

>>> print ('This is an example of calling the Prod function with two integers:', A)

This is an example of calling the Prod function with two integers: 6

>>> A = Prod (1.5, 3)

>>> print ('This is an example of calling the Prod function with a float and integer:', A)

This is an example of calling the Prod function with a float and integer: 4.5

>>> A = Prod ('name', 3)

>>> print ('This is an example of calling the Prod function with a string and integer\n:', A)

This is an example of calling the Prod function with a string and integer:

namenamename

>>> A = Prod ('name', 'name')

Traceback (most recent call last):

 File "<stdin>", line 1, in <module>

 File "<stdin>", line 2, in Prod

 TypeError: can't multiply sequence by non-int of type 'str'

In the examples above, we called the function and passed two integers, a float and integer, and a string and an integer. In the first case, it returned an integer. In the second, it returned a float, and in the third, it returned a string. In the final example, we passed two strings input arguments and Python raised an error because multiplication between strings does not exit. Overall, there is no declaration or restriction on the data type that can be passed to a function as long as the operations in the function body are defined.

Overall, Python functions allow defining code scripts that are reusable as many times as it is needed. There are no restrictions on the data object type passed as arguments. The code becomes general and used in any context as long as the operations inside the function are defined. Moreover, you can define your own operations inside these functions or include exception statements that can handle issues in this case. By coding a script within a function, it makes it easy to make a modification if needed and to be made in one single place. You can also insert a function code within a module file.

This way, the function can be imported by importing the module and used within any program or shared with other programs for wide broad use. In fact, this is exactly how packages are developed and used in Python. In the next chapter, we are going to cover this specific topic on how to develop modules with Python.

Chapter 6: Modules in Python

Modules, also known as packages, are a set of names. This is usually a library of functions and/or object classes that are made available to be used within different programs. We used the notion of modules earlier in this chapter to use some function from the math library. In this chapter, we are going to cover in-depth on how to develop and define modules. In order to use modules in a Python program, the following statements are used: import, from, reload. The first one imports the whole module. The second allows import only a specific name or element from the module. The third one, reload, allows reloading a code of a module while Python is running and without stopping in it. Before digging into their definition and development, let's start first by the utility of modules or packages within Python.

Modules Concept and Utility Within Python

Modules are a very simple way to make a system component organized. Basically, modules allow reusing the same code over and over. So far, we were working in a Python interactive session. Every code we have written and tested is lost once we exit the interactive session. Modules are saved in files that make them persistent, reusable, and sharable. You can consider modules as a set of files where you can define functions, names, data objects, attributes, and so on. Modules are a tool to group several components of a system in a single place. In Python programming, modules are among the highest-level unit.

They point to the name of packages and tools. In addition, they allow the sharing of the implemented data. You only need one copy of the module to be able to use across a large program. If an object is to be used in different functions and programs, coding it as a module allows share it with other programmers.

To have a sense of the architecture of Python coding, we go through some general structure explanation. We have been using so far in this book very simple code examples that do not really have high-level structure. In large applications, a program is a set of several Python files. By Python files, we mean files that contain Python code and have a .py extension. There is one main high-level program and the other files are the modules. The high-level file consists of the main code that dictates the control flow and executes the application. Module files define the tools that are needed to process elements and components of the main program and maybe elsewhere. The main program makes use of the tools that are specified in the modules.

In their turn, modules make use of tools that are specified in other modules. When you import a module in Python, you have access to every tool that is declared or defined in that specific module. Attributes are the variables or the functions associated with the tools within a module. Hence, when a module is imported, we have access to the attributes of the tools as well to process them.

For instance, let's consider we have two Python files named file1.py and file2.py where the file1.py is the main program and file2.py is the module. In the file2.py, we have a code that defines the following function that we have used in the previous chapter:

```
def Xfactorial (X):
    P = 1
    for i in range (1, X + 1):
        P *= i
    return P
```

In order to use this function in the main program, we should define code statements in the file1.py as follows:

```
Import file2
A = file2.Xfactorial (3)
```

The first line imports the module file2.py. This statement means to load the file file2.py.
This gives access to the file1.py to all tools and functions defined in file2.py by the name file2. The function Xfactorial is called by the second line. The module file2.py is where this function is defined using the attributes' syntax. The line file2.Xfactorial() means fetch any name value of Xfactorial and lies within the code body of file2. In this example, it is a function that is callable. So, we have provided an input argument and assigned the output result to the variable A. If we add a third statement to print the variable A and run the file file1.py, it would display 6 which is the factorial of 3. Along Python, you will see the attribute syntax as object.attribute. This basically allows calling the attributes that might be a function or data object that provides properties of the object.

Note that some modules that you might import when programming with Python are available in Python itself. As we have mentioned at the beginning of this book, Python comes with a standard large library that has built-in modules. These modules support all common tasks that might be needed in programming from operating system interfaces to graphical user interface. They are not part of the language. However, they can be imported and comes with a software installation package. You can check the complete list of available modules in a manual that comes with the installation or goes to the official Python website: www.Python.org. This manual is kept updated every time a new version of Python is released.

How to Import a Module

We have talked about importing a module without really explaining what happens behind in Python. Imports are a very fundamental concept in Python programming structure. In this section, we are going to cover in-depth how really Python imports modules within a program. In fact, Python follows three steps to import a file or a module within the work environment of a program. The first step consists of finding the file that contains the module. The second step consists of compiling the module to a byte-code if required. Finally, the third step runs the code within the module file in order to build the objects that are defined. These three steps are run only when the module is imported for the first time during the execution of a program.

This module and all its objects are loaded in the memory. When the module is imported further in the program, it skips all three steps and just fetch the objects defined by the module and are saved in memory. At the very first step of importing a module, Python has to find the module file location.

Note that, so far in the examples we presented, we used import without providing the complete path of the module or extension .py. We just used import math, or import file2.py (an example of the previous section). Python import statement omits the extension and the path. We just simply import a module by its name. The reason for this is that Python has a module that looks for paths called 'search path module'. This module is used specifically to find the path of module files that are imported by the import statements.

In some cases, you might need to configure the path search of modules in order to be able to use new modules that are not part of the standard library. You need to customize it in order to include these new modules. The search path is simply the concatenation of the home directory, directories of PYTHONPATH, directories of the standard library, and optionally if the content of files with extension .pth when they exist. The home directory is set automatically by the system to a directory of Python executable when launched from the interactive session, or it can be modified to the working directory where your program is saved.
This directory is the first to be searched when import a module is run without a path. Hence, if your home directory points to a directory that includes your program along with the modules, importing these modules does not require any path specification.

The directory of the standard library is also searched automatically. This directory contains all default libraries that come with Python. The directories of PYTHONPATH can be set in order to point toward the directory of new modules that are developed. In fact, PTYHONPATH is an environment variable that contains a list of directories that contains Python files. When PTYHONPATH is set, all these paths are included in the Python environment and the search path directory would search these directories too when importing modules. Python also allows defining a file with .pth extension that contains directories, one in each line. This file serves the same as PTYHONPATH when included appropriately in a directory. You can check the directories' paths included when you run Python using sys.path.

You simply print sys.path to get the list of the directories that Python will be searching for.

Remember, when importing a module, we just use the name of the module without its extension. When Python is searching for a module in its environment paths, it selects the first name that matches the module name regardless of the extension. Because Python allows using packages that are coded in other languages, it does not simply select a module with .py extension but a file name or even a zip file name that matches the module name being imported. Therefore, you should name your modules distinctly and configure the search path in a manner that makes it obvious to choose a module.

When Python finds the source code of the module file with a name that corresponds to the name in the import statement, it will compile it into byte code in case it is required. This step is skipped if Python finds an already byte code file with no source code.

If the source code has been modified, another byte code file is automatically regenerated by Python while the program runs in other further executions. Byte code files have typically .pyc extension. When Python is searching and finds the module file name, it will load the byte code file that corresponds to the latest version of the source code with .py extension.

If the source code is newer than the byte code file, it will generate a new one by compiling the source code file. Note that only imported files have corresponding files with .pyc extension. These files, the byte code files, are stored on your machine to make the imports faster in future use. The third step of the import statement is running the module's byte code. Each statement and each assignment in the file are executed. This allows generating any function, data objects, and so on defined in the module. The functions and all attributes are accessed within the program via importers. During this step, you will see print statements if they exist. The 'def ' statement will create a function object to be used in the main program.

To summarize the import statement, involve searching for the file, compiling it, and running the byte code file. All other imports statement uses the module stored in memory and ignore all the three steps. When first imported, Python will look in the search path module to select the module. Hence, it is important to configure correctly the path environment variable to point to the directory that contains new defined modules. Now that you have the big picture and the concept of modules, let's explore how we can define and develop new modules.

How to write and use a module in Python?

Modules in Python can be created very easily and do not require any specific syntax. Modules are simply files with a .py extension that contains Python code. You can use a text editor like Notepad++ to develop and write modules then save them in files with the .py extension. Then, you just import these files like we have seen in the previous section to make use of the contained code.

When you create a module, all the data object including functions that are defined becomes the module attributes. These attributes are accessed and used via the attribute syntax like follows: module.attribute. For instance, if we define a module named ' MyModule.py ' that has the following function:

```
def Myfct (A):
        print (' A by 2 is: ', A * 2)
        return A * 2
```

The function ' Myfct ' becomes the attribute of the module ' MyModule.py '. Basically, you can call a module any Python code that you develop and save in a file with a .py extension if you are importing them in later use. Module names are referenced variables. Hence, when naming a module, you should follow the same rules as for variable naming. You might be able to name your module anything you want. But if the rules are not respected, Python throws an error. For instance, if you name your module $2P.py, you will not be able to import it and Python would trigger a syntax error.

Directory names that contain the module and Python packages should follow the same rules. In addition, their names cannot contain any space. In the rest of this section, we are going to provide some code examples of defining and using modules.

There are two statements that can be employed to make use of a module. The first one is the import statement we have covered in the previous section. Let's consider again the previous example to illustrate a module 'MyModule.py' that contains ' Myfct' function:

```
def Myfct(A):
        print (A, 'by 2 is: ', A * 2)
```

Now, to use this module, we import it using the following statements:

```
>>> import MyModule
>>> MyModule.Myfct(2)
2 by 2 is: 4
```

Now, the MyModule name is being used by Python to load the file and as a variable in the program. The module name should be used to access all its attributes. Another way to import and use a module attribute is by using the 'from import' statement.

This statement works in the same manner as the import statement we have been using. Instead of using the module name to fetch for its attributes, we can access the attributes by their names directly.
For example:

>>> from MyModule import Myfct

>>> Myfct (2)

2 by 2 is: 4

Basically, this statement makes a copy of the function name without using the module name. There is another form of 'from import' statement that uses an *. This statement allows copying all names that are assigned to objects in the module. For example:

>>> from MyModule import *

>>> Myfct (2)

2 by 2 is: 4

Because modules names become variables (i.e. references to objects), Python supports importing a module with an alias. Then we can access its attributes using the alias instead of its name.

For instance, we can attribute an alias to our module like follows:

```
>>> import Mymodule as md
>>> md.Myfct(2)
2 by 2 is: 4
```

Data objects other than functions are accessed the same way with attribute syntax. For instance, we can define and initialize data objects in modules than used them later in the program. Let's consider the following code to create a module named ExModule.py.

```
A = 9
Name = 'John'
```

In this example, we initialize both variables A and Name. Now, after importing the module, we can get both variables as follows:

```
>>> import ExModule
>>> print ('A is: ', ExModule.A)
A is: 9
>>> print ('Name is: ', Exmodule.Name)
Name is: John
```

Or we can assign the attributes to other variables. For instance:

```
>>> import ExModule
>>> B = ExModule.A
>>> print ('B is: ', B)
B is: 9
```

If we use the 'from import' statement to import the attributes, the names of the attributes become variables in the script.

For example:

```
>>> from Exmodule import A, Name
>>> print ('A is: ', A, 'and Name is: ', Name)
A is 9 and Name is John
```

Note that from the import statement supports importing multiple attributes in one single line. Python allows changing objects that are sharable. For instance, let's consider the following code to define the module named ExModul1.py:

```
A = 9
MyList = [ 90, 40, 80]
```

Now, let's import this module and try to change the values of the attributes to see how Python behaves.

```
>>> from ExModule1 import A, MyList
>>> A = 20
>>> myList [ 0] = 100
```

Now, let's re-import the module and print those two attributes and see what changes Python has made.

```
>>> import ExModule1
>>> print (' A is: ', ExModule1.A)
A is: 9
>>> print ('My list is: ', ExModule.myList)
My list is: [100, 40, 80]
```

You can notice that Python has changed the value of the first element of the list but did not change the value of the variable 'A' to the value we assigned before. The reason is that when a mutable object like lists is changed locally, the changes apply also in the module from which they were imported. Reassigning a fetched variable name does not reassign the reference in the module from which it was imported. In fact, there is no link between the reference variable name copied and the file it was copied from. In order to make a valid modification in the script and the module it is imported from, we should use the import statement like follows:

145

```
>>> import ExModule1

>>> ExModule1.A = 200
```

The difference between changing the attributes 'A' and 'myList' is the fact that 'A' is a variable name and 'myList' is an object data. That is why modification to the variable 'A' should use import to be applied in the module file, too.

We have mentioned that importing a module for the first time in a script implies going through three steps that are searching for the module, compiling the module, and running the module. All other imports of the module later in the script skip all these three steps and access to module loaded in the memory. Now, let's try an example to see how this really works. Consider we have a module with the following code and named ExModule2.py:

```
print (' Hello World\n')

print (' This is my first module in Python')

A = 9
```

Now, let's import this module and see how Python behaves when importing this module:

```
>>> import ExModule2

Hello World

This is my first module in Python

>>>
```

You can notice that when importing this module, it displays both messages. Now, let's try to reassign a value to the attribute ' A', then re-import the module with the import statement.

```
>>> ExModule.A = 100
>>> import Exmodule2
>>>
```

As you can note from the example, Python did not display the messages, ' Hello World' and ' This is my first module in Python' because it did not re-run the module. It just used the module that is already loaded in the memory.

In order to make Python really goes through all steps of importing a module for the second time in a script, we should use the reload statement. When using this statement, we force Python to import the module as it would for the first time. In addition, it helps make modifications in the program while it is running without interrupting it. It also helps see instantly the modifications that are made. The reload is actually a function and not a statement in Python that takes as argument a module that is already loaded in memory.

Because reload is a function and expects an argument, this argument should be already assigned an object which is a module object. If for some reason the import statement failed to import a module, you will not be able to reload it. You have to repeat the import statement until it imports the module successfully. Like any other function, the reload takes the module name reference between parenthesis.

The general form of using reload with import is as follows:

```
import module_name
list of statements that use module attributes
reload(module_name)
list of statements that use module attributes
```

The module object is changed by the reload function. Hence, any reference to that module in your scripts is impacted by the reload function. Those statements that use the module attributes will be using the values of the new attributes if they are modified. The reload function overwrites the module source code and re-runs it instead of deleting the file and creating a new one. In the following code example, we will see a concrete illustration of the reload functioning. We consider the following code to create a module named ExModule3.py:

```
my_message = ' This is my module first version'
def display ():
        print (my_message)
```

This module simply assigns a string to the variable 'my_message' and print it.

Now, let's import this module in Python and call the attribute function:

```
>>> import ExModule3
>>> Exmodule3.display()
This is my module first version
>>>
```

Now, go to your text editor and edit the module source code without stopping the Python prompt shell.

You can make a change as follows:

```
my_message = ' This is my module second version edited in the
text editor'
def display ():
        print (my_message)
```

Now, back to the interactive session of Python in the prompt shell, you can try to import the module and call the function:

```
>>> import ExModule3
>>> Exmodule3.display()
This is my module first version
>>>
```

As you can notice that the message did not change although the source code file was modified. As said before, all imports after the first import use the already loaded module in memory. To get the new message and access the modification made in the module, we use the reload function:

>>> reload (ExModule3)

<module 'ExModule3)>

>>> Exmodule3.display()

This is my module second version edited in the text editor

Note that the reload function re-runs module and returns the module object.
Because it was executed in the interactive session, it displays < module name> by default.

Chapter 7: Python Debugging

In some cases, a program is developed, but when running, it does not provide the desired outcome or it gets stuck somewhere in the workflow. This implies that the program should be scrutinized while it is running on a test in order to get a sense of where the program should be corrected or where things go wrong. This action is what is named by programmers debugging. This task is actively used in order to make sure that a program is running as it is supposed to be. In this chapter, we will cover this topic and present the commands that are available to debug Python programs. First, let's talk in-depth about what is debugging.

What is debugging?

Debugging is simply the process of finding and fixing errors in a program. Debugging verifies the functioning of a program to fix statements of operations that make the program stack and not running appropriately.

The simplest and most obvious way to debug a program is using the print function in order to spot the output of functions or variables. In general, the print allows getting information to have a look inside of the functioning of the program. However, this method has several drawbacks. The major is that you need to add changes to the code several times in order to add the print in places where you need to extract information. These places are commonly known as breakpoints. Then you have to run the program every time. There are some advanced debugger tools that can be used.

These tools mostly are very efficient and allow saving a great amount of time when used compared to debugging with print. Python has a debugger that comes by default with the software when installed. This debugger is simply a tool that gives ways to get a look at the code while it is running. When using this tool, you can make changes instantly in the code and alter the values of the variables all while you run the code in chunks. The debugger that comes with Python is named pdb. This tool is in the form of a command-line interface.

This debugger, as any package, is imported with the import statement in order to be able to use it.

```
import pdb, pdb.set_trace.
```

In order to be used, the debugger should be imported into the program you wish to debug. When Python interpreter runs this line, you will be redirected to a prompt command on your terminal in which the program is launched. Typically, this is the prompt of Python with commands that allows you to evaluate your code. We cover the list of these commands in the following section.

Python Debugger Commands

Python default debugger has several debugging commands which are presented in the table below. Here we cover the most basic one. The first command, list, allows you to list the line where the control workflow is on. You can check specific parts of your code by passing their first and last lines as arguments to the list command.

You can also check the code around a specific line bypassing only the number of this line to the list command. The up and down commands allow navigating around the code of your program. By using these commands, you are able to know which statement is calling the function that is currently running or understand reasons why the interpreter is behaving or running certain code parts. The next and step are commands that allow resuming execution of the code line by line. The next command will jump to the following line of the function that is currently running even if it calls another function. On the contrary, the step function allows you to go deeper in the code chain rather than just executing the following line. Finally, the break is a command that enables adding new breakpoints with no requirements to make any modifications in the source code.

Table 9: List Python debugger commands

Debug command	Explanation
Alias or a	allows creating an alias to the command
args or rgs	allows showing the list of arguments
break or b	allows setting breakpoints.
disable	allows disabling breakpoints supplied as a list separated by a space
ignore	allows setting a count for a number of breakpoints
commands	allows specifying a command list for a number of breakpoints

continue or c or cont	continue running the code until it reaches a breakpoint
exit	quit the debugger
interact	launch an interpreter that is interactive
list or l	allows showing the code for specific lines
next or n	resumes execution until the following line of the function currently running
restart	allows restarting the program
step or s	run expression in the current line
unalias	removes alias
where or w	displays a trace of the recent last frame
down or d	goes to the next line down
up or u	goes to the above line
clear or cl	allows clearing all breakpoints
enable	allows enabling breakpoints
condition	allows setting conditions for breakpoints as a test that should be evaluated to true in order to set the breakpoint
p	allows evaluating the expression in the current line
help or h	If no argument is supplied, displays list of commands, otherwise, displays information about the command passed as

	an argument
jump or j	allows setting the number of the line to run next; it allows jumping code parts or running the code from the start
longlist or ll	allows showing the whole code for the function currently running
quit or q	exit the debugger and abort the program
return or r	continue running the code until hits a function return
tbreak	allows making a temporary breakpoint
until or ill	if no argument is passed, it continues running the code until a line which has a number superior to the current is reached
whatis	displays the expression type

Now that you know the concept behind debugging and its basic commands, let's see a real example.

We consider the following code saved in a file named test.py.

```
def Myfct1 (A):
        print ('A by 2 is:', A * 2)
    return A * 2


def Myfct2 (B, A):
        C = B * A
    A = 4
    B = 'name'
    Myfct2 (B, A)
```

You can notice that this code does not import Python debugger, the pdb module. Instead, we are going to launch the function in the prompt with Python in a debugger mode with the following command:

```
C:\Users\***\Desktop>Python -m pdb test.py
> c:\users\***\desktop\test.py(1)<module>()
-> def Myfct (A):
(Pdb)
```

As you can see, Python did not return the usual >>> in the prompt but it returned instead (Pdb). This means that the debugger is waiting for debugger commands. Now, let's test some of the commands listed in Table 9 above to get a sense of how the debugger works.

We start by the list command.

```
(Pdb) list
1 -> def Myfct1(A):
2 print ('A by 2 is:', A * 2)
3 return A * 2
4
5 def Myfct2(B, A):
6 C = B * A
7
8 A = 4
9 B = 'name'
10 Myfct2(B, A)
[EOF]
```

In this example, we applied the list command with no argument. It returned the content of the file with line numbers. If we pass arguments (i.e. line numbers) to the list command, it will return only the code that shows between these lines.

For instance:

```
(Pdb) list 2, 3
 2 print ('A by 2 is:', A * 2)
 3 return A * 2
(Pdb)
```

If we use now the next command it will return, the next line after where the current curser is:

```
(Pdb) next
> c:\users\***\desktop\test.py(5)<module>()
-> def Myfct2(B, A):
(Pdb)
```

We skip lines in the debugger using the jump command as follows:

```
(Pdb) jump 8
> c:\users\*****\desktop\test.py(8)<module>()
-> A = 4
(Pdb)
```

If we try to print the variable 'A', Python will display a name error because this statement is not yet executed. The curser is just pointing to this line:

```
(Pdb) A
*** NameError: name 'A' is not defined
(Pdb)
```

Now, in order to print variable names, we should actually run the program with commands that actually run the program not just show its content. Among these commands is the continue command.

So, let's run now the continue command:

```
(Pdb) continue
Traceback (most recent call last):
    File "C:\Users\****\Anaconda3\lib\pdb.py", line 1697, in main
pdb._runscript(mainpyfile)
    File "C:\Users\****\Anaconda3\lib\pdb.py", line 1566, in _runscript
    self.run(statement)
    File "C:\Users\****\Anaconda3\lib\bdb.py", line 585, in run
exec (cmd, globals, locals)
File "<string>", line 1, in <module>
File "c:\users\****\desktop\test.py", line 8, in <module>
A = 4
NameError: name 'Myfct2' is not defined
Uncaught exception. Entering post mortem debugging
Running 'cont' or 'step' will restart the program
> c:\users\*****\desktop\test.py(8)<module>()
-> A = 4
```

Now, here that the continue launched different built-in functions of the debugger. It finally displayed an Error name for the 'Myfct2' because the 'def' statement of this function was not executed. Now, if we try to print the value of the variable ' A ', we get:

```
(Pdb) A
4
(Pdb)
```

If we reach the bottom of the file and run, for instance, the next command, Python debugger returns:

```
(Pdb) next
Post mortem debugger finished. The test.py will be restarted
> c:\users\***\desktop\test.py(1)<module>()
-> def Myfct1(A):
```

The longlist command allows showing the entire code. For instance:

```
(Pdb) longlist
1 -> def Myfct1 (A):
2 print ('A by 2 is:', A*2)
3 return A * 2
4
5 def Myfct2 (B, A):
6 C = B * A
7
8 A = 4
9 B = 'name'
10 Myfct2(B, A)
(Pdb)
```

Now, to run a code, we use the command step. For instance, let's quit the debugger with the command q() and restarted it again to test the command step.

```
(Pdb) q()
C:\Users\****\Desktop>Python -m pdb test.py
> c:\users\****\desktop\test.py(1)<module>()
-> def Myfct1 (A):
(Pdb) step
> c:\users\****\desktop\test.py(5)<module>()
-> def Myfct2 (B, A):
(Pdb)
```

As you can notice, when a step command is run, the current line is def Myfct2 (B, A). This means that it is executed the 'def' statement of the first function. We can test that by calling this function:

```
(Pdb) Myfct1 (3)
A by 2 is: 6
6
(Pdb)
```

We can also pass an argument to step function to specify which line to run. For instance, we pass as argument Line 8. The debugger will run everything before line 8.

As we can see from the example below, we can both print the variable A and call the function Myfct2 because these statements were both executed.

```
(Pdb) step 8
> c:\users\****\desktop\test.py(8)<module>()
-> B = 'name'
(Pdb) A
4
 (Pdb) Myfct2 (5, 3)
(Pdb)
```

Because we have reached the end of the file, let's use continue to go back to the beginning of the file and test other commands.

```
(Pdb) cont
The program finished and will be restarted
> c:\users\****\desktop\test.py(1)<module>()
-> def Myfct1 (A):
```

As you can see when running continue command at the end file, the debugger shows a message that lets you know that the program has finished and it is restarting. Now, we are going to test the whatis command:

```
(Pdb) whatis 2
<class 'int'>
(Pdb)
```

This command returns the type of the data object of the expression that appears in the Line passed as an argument.

Now, let's set some breakpoints using the command break.

```
(Pdb) break 3

Breakpoint 1 at c:\users\*****\desktop\test.py:3

(Pdb)
```

This command displays a message regarding where the breakpoint was added along with the Python file.
We can clear breakpoints with the clear command. After running this command, the debugger will display a message that asks whether you want to clear all breaks or not. Then it prints a message to confirm that the breakpoint was deleted along with the path of the Python file.

```
(Pdb) clear

Clear all breaks? Y

Deleted breakpoint 1 at c:\users\****\desktop\test.py:3

(Pdb)
```

If you run a longlist after adding a breakpoint in your Python script, it will show you where the breakpoint was added. So, you don't have to go check in your Text Editor.

For instance, we add a break in line number 2:

```
(Pdb) break 2
Breakpoint 2 at c:\users\****\desktop\test.py:2
(Pdb) longlist
 1 def Myfct1 (A):
 2 B print ('A by 2 is:', A * 2)
 3 return A * 2
 4
 5 def Myfct2 (B, A):
 6 C = B * A
 7 A = 4
 8 B = 'name'
 9 -> Myfct2 (B,A)
(Pdb)
```

To resume this chapter, using debugger tools are very efficient to get a look inside of the program while it is running. It let you know what's going on when the program is running without having to make any changes in its source code. In addition, you can see all the changes you make and breakpoints you add while you are debugging with the Python module pdb.

Moreover, this Python default debugger has numerous commands listed in Table 9 that allows an efficient scrutinization of your code.

Chapter 8: Files in Python

Files are a wide notion that is used to call any storage of your computer and handled by the operating system. Files are used to store data and information. When programming, you need tools that extract this information from the files or tools to save processed information in a file. In this chapter, we are going to cover how to handle files in Python.

Reading and writing files in Python

In Python, files are considered as a data object. In fact, Python has a built-in data object type assigned specifically for files. Unlike other data types we have seen in chapter 3, the file data object is associated only with common methods used to process files. The built-in method open is a function that allows creating a file data object to be processed. In short, this method links the file data object to the file stored in the hardware of your machine. Once you call open function, you have access to the file in order to read it or write it using the read and write attributes of the file data object.

Table 10 presented below lists all common methods used to process files. In order to read a file, the function open is called with file name along with the mode to process the file which is 'r' in this case. To write a file, the process mode is 'w'. This mode creates a new file. If a file exists with the same name used to open a file in a writing mode, it will be overwritten. In order to write or add content into the existing file, the file should be open with mode append (i.e. 'a').

The file name can include or not the file path of the directory that contains or will contain the file. If the path is not specified, then Python would assume that the file is in the working directory which is the directory where the current program is running.

Table 10: List methods to process files.

Method	Explanation
File2Read = open (file_path/file_name, 'r')	Defines a file data object to write
File2write = open (file_path/file_name, 'w')	Defines a file data object to read
content = File2read.read()	Reads the whole file and assign the content to a single string
content = File2read.read(X)	Reads only X bytes
Line = File2read.readLine()	Reads following line
Lines = File2read.readLins()	Reads the whole file and stores the content in a line strings list
File2write(data)	Writes data in the file
File2write.writeLine(List_line)	Writes in the file the strings line of the list List_line
File2write.close()	Closes the file manually

After you open a file, you have a file data object. Then, its methods can be used in reading and writing with the methods presented in the table above. In either case, the file data object methods take and return only strings in Python. In other words, the read method returns as a data object type as a string. The write method takes as data object type as string, too. Both methods have different varieties.

The role of the close method is closing the connection between Python and the external file residing in the hardware of your machine. Python also liberates the space in memory that was occupied by an object after it is no longer referenced in the script. Python would also close automatically the close if required. Hence, in Python, it is not necessary to call the close method in order to delete the file object reference manually. However, it is good practice to call the close method after you finish reading or writing a file.

Example File Processing in Python

In this section, we are going to present some examples of processing files in Python using the methods presented in Table 10. The first example illustrates how to write the 'Hello World' in a file. So, let's go back to prompt shell and launch Python for practice.

```
>>> File = open (' MyFile.txt', 'w')
>>> File.write(' Hello World! \n')
>>> File.close()
```

In the first statement, we called the method open in write mode (i.e. 'w') to create the file. The second statement writes the line 'Hello World!' with a newline marker. The third statement closes the file object.

In the following code example, we are going to open the file in reading mode (i.e. 'r') and get the line written in the file:

```
>>> File = open (' MyFile.txt', 'r')
>>> A = File.readline()
>>> print (' This is an example of reading a file with readline: \n', A)
This is an example of reading a file with readline:
Hello World!
>>> File.close()
```

Now, we are going to add a second line in our file. To do so, we are going to open the file in mode append (i.e. 'a') and write the line 'My first file in Python':

```
>>> File = open (' MyFile.txt', 'a')
>>> File.write(' This is my first file in Python')
>>> File.close()
```

If we open the file again and check its content with the read method, we get the following output:

```
>>> File = open (' MyFile.txt', 'r')
>>> A = File.read()
>>> print (' This is an example of reading a file with read: \n', A)
This is an example of reading a file with read:
Hello World!
This is my first file in Python
>>> File.close()
```

As you can notice when opening a file with append mode, it adds whatever you write in the file at the end. We can also change what is already in the file by opening the file in mode 'r+'. When you open the file in this mode and write in it, it will overwrite everything in it.

For instance:

```
>>> File = open (' MyFile.txt', 'r+')
>>> File.write(' This is my first file Python opened in mode r+')
>>> File.close()
>>> File = open (' MyFile.txt', 'r')
>>> A = File.read()
>>> print (' Checking file after opening in mode r+: \n', A)
Checking file after opening in mode r+:
This is my first file Python opened in mode r+
>>>File.close()
```

Remember, loops are very handy when it comes to repeating the same tasks for a specific number of times. In particular, loops are very useful in processing the file data object. We have seen through the above examples that we can read the content of the whole file in one single step using the read method. In some cases, we need to read the file line by line. In this case, we would use the readLine method. We might also need to write the file line by line in the case of formatted files, in which case, the writelines is handy. Let's practice some examples.

First, we are going to write using writelines method. Then we are going to read the same file line by line. For both tasks, we will use a while loop.

```
>>> List_string = [' This is an example of \n',
... 'writing a file \n',
... ' on multiple lines\n',
... ' using write Lines \n',
... ' inside a while loop']
>>>print (' List of strings is:\n ', List_string)
List of strings is:
[' This is an example of \n', 'writing a file \n', ' on multiple lines\n', ' using write Lines', ' inside a while loop']
>>> File = open ('Test', 'w')
>>> File.writelines (List_string)
>>> File.close ()
```

Remember that all file object methods process only strings. Therefore, we created a list of strings where each element end with /n for newline maker.

Now, we open the file for reading:

```
>>> File = open ('Test', 'r')
>>> while 1:
...        Line = File.readline ()
...        if not Line: break
...         print (Line)
...
This is an example of
writing a file
on multiple lines
using write Lines inside a while loop
>>> File.close ()
```

As you can notice, we have a break statement in the while loop. This ensures that the while loop stops when there is no line to read. In other words, it ensures that the loop exit when it reaches the end of the file. Because 1 is always evaluated to true, the loop will continue running until it runs to the break. Hence, this loop reads the file line by line until it reaches the end of the file.

If we open the file and use the read method, we get exactly the same results:

```
>>> File = open ('Test', 'r')
>>> A = File.read ()
>>> print ('This is the output from reading the file with reading
method: \n', A)
This is the output from reading the file with reading method:
This is an example of
writing a file
on multiple lines
using write Lines inside a while loop
>>> File.close ()
```

Note in this last example, we did not specify the file extension. In fact, Python allows handling and processing any type of files that the extension does not matter. These methods work the same on any file.

Conclusion

Thank you for making it through to the end of *Python Programming: A Comprehensive Smart Approach for Total Beginners to Learn Python Language Using Best Practices And Advanced Features*. Let's hope it was informative and able to provide you with all of the tools you need to achieve your goals whatever they may be.

This book provides the basics of Python language programming. It also covers some advanced topics such as developing modules, debugging, and handling files. This book does not require any programming prerequisites. On the contrary, this book is designed to provide total beginners with the right tools to start programming using the Python language.

In the very first chapters, chapter 1 to chapter 3, we cover the most basics of any programming language which are how to install the language and how to run scripts. We also cover the data object type and how to process them.

In chapter 4, we start diving into more details about Python syntax, operators, and if test and loops specifics to process data objects. In the rest of the book, we cover more advanced topics such as developing functions and modules to make any script reusable and widely sharable with others. We also cover debugging which allows finding and fixing code errors, and finally, how to process files. All chapters of this book provide code examples that allow practicing while you are learning the language.

After finishing this book, you will not only be able to develop scripts to accomplish simple tasks, but you will be also able to develop your own modules. You will also be able to use these modules within any program. In short, you will be able to master basic programming with Python with some advanced features. You will also be able to debug and scrutinize your programs while they are running. Once you master these skills, you will be able to pick up more advanced skills easily.

Finally, if you found this book useful in any way, a review on Amazon is always appreciated!

Python Machine Learning

Understand Python Libraries (Keras, NumPy, Scikit-lear, TensorFlow) for Implementing Machine Learning Models in Order to Build Intelligent Systems

By: Ethem Mining

Introduction

For decades, artificial intelligence has been more promise than delivery. With the advent of increasing computing power and the arrival of big data, however, things have started to change. Over the past 15 years or so, a new and relatively quiet revolution began in the area of artificial intelligence. Finally, the hype began to meet with the substance. It should be made clear that the old visions of human-like robots running around and eventually displacing humans still remain quite far-fetched. What we are seeing instead is that computers are doing what they've always done, helping aid humans working in areas where humans aren't really that suitable. Nonetheless, the impact on business over the past decade has been enormous, and more big changes are ahead.

In this book, we hope to get the reader interested in and informed about a branch of artificial intelligence called machine learning. The aim of this guide is to get you acquainted with some of the tools used in machine learning that make it accessible and practical. Those who become familiar with the python libraries and tools that can be used in machine learning are going to find it surprisingly easy to use.

We will begin the book with some background material, to make sure that all readers are on the same page. First, we will introduce the concept of machine learning and explain what it's all about, and how it can be applied in the real world.

Then we will discuss the two main types of machine learning, supervised and unsupervised machine learning. From there, we will describe the tools available in python that can be used to do machine learning.

Python is very accessible and easy language to learn. If you are not familiar with python, there are many fine books on the topic, and you can find many websites that will teach you how to use the language.

Those who already have experience with computer programming will find that using python is comparatively easy as compared to most programming languages.

There are plenty of books on this subject on the market, thanks again for choosing this one! Every effort was made to ensure it is full of as much useful information as possible, please enjoy it!

Chapter 9: An Introduction to Machine Learning

Artificial intelligence is a branch of computer science that seeks to develop computer systems that are capable of humanlike intelligence. This is something that can be viewed from many different directions. The first thing that might come to mind when you think of human intelligence is that it is general in nature. You can learn to do many different things, from mathematics to learning a new language, or visual recognition.

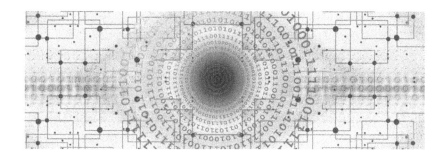

The second aspect of human intelligence that is important is that humans learn from experience. As we will see, this is going to be a critical aspect of machine learning. The experience that you learn from might come in different forms. You can learn by doing, or you can be guided through learning by an instructor. One way you learn is by memorizing, which is a form of experience.

The key point here is that the human brain adjusts itself, basically restructuring itself, when it is exposed to new information. In the end, whether or not you are learning how to play tennis or do calculus, everything is basically information of some kind.

Of course, human intelligence can be broken down into specialties, so you can have artificial intelligence that replicates the human mind implemented this way rather than just having a computer system that mimics and the entire human brain. In fact, the latter is probably something very far off, if it is ever achieved. However, artificially intelligent computer systems are quite good at performing specialized tasks. Computer vision, for example, is one area that has taken off and continues to get better and better.

Artificially intelligent systems also run independently. Think of it as educating a child in school. The child is taught in school, and when they become an adult, they become an independent operator. Most adult humans don't need to consult their teachers or parents all the time in order to make decisions. Computer systems based on artificial intelligence need to be trained, but once trained they can operate on their own without human intervention.

Another aspect of human intelligence can be captured by the phrase "practice makes perfect". Or put another way, the more data you are exposed to the better you get at solving problems related to that data. Computer systems based on artificial intelligence get better at what they do the more data they are exposed to. They self-adjust to make themselves perform better.

This is quite a contrast with conventional computer systems, which can do a lot of powerful things, but are essentially dumb. They only do what you tell them to do, and without humans rewriting the programs that run them, they don't get any better at what they do. This is an important point to focus on, because the kinds of systems that we are going to talk about in this book will adjust themselves and get better, without any human intervention whatsoever. Once they are deployed, the human operators might not even understand why the artificially intelligent computer system makes the decisions it does, or how it is making those decisions. The worth of the systems can only be judged on results alone.

What is Machine Learning and How Has it Developed?

Machine learning is actually an old technology, as far as computer technology is concerned. The first machine learning system was constructed in the mid-to-late 1950s. It was developed at IBM, and described in a paper published in the peer reviewed literature. This system was able to learn how to play checkers. The system has some key components that make us recognize it as machine learning.

The first item to note is that the system was not designed to play checkers. Instead, the system was designed to learn, and to self-adapt. It learned to play checkers by being exposed to playing checkers.

The second item to consider is that the more the system played checkers, the better it got. This is an illustration of the ability of these types of computer systems to benefit from the experience. Just like a human being, the more experience they have at doing something, the better they get.

There is one key aspect that you should be aware of when considering a program like this. A human being can learn to play checkers, and they can also learn to play monopoly and guitar. Although years ago researchers in the field hoped to build computers that were like this too, the machine learning systems in use today are not like that. In short, they are one trick ponies. So, our system that we are describing here was really good at playing checkers. It could not do anything else. Once you have a system that does something, that is what it does, period.

With the first system built some 60 odd years ago, you might be wondering why it is only recently that this type of computer system has become relevant to the real world. There are two reasons. One is the messy way that research develops in any human enterprise. A few years after this development, computer scientists got extremely hot on the idea of general artificial intelligence. Huge promises were made, and lots of hype developed around the field. This was when the idea of fully functioning "android" robots caught fire.

These would be human-like computer systems packaged in a human-like form, often indistinguishable from humans. The movie Alien captured this idea quite well with the ship scientist named Ash; the other crew members didn't even know he was an android.

The idea of artificial intelligence was also portrayed in the famous science fiction movie 2001: A Space Odyssey.

This was a more realistic portrayal, the computer was not human-like in form, but it clearly had a mind. One of the key themes in the film is the fact that the system has faults, and can make bad decisions as a result. This is probably a warning we should take to heart, but we probably won't. The system in the movie brags that it never makes mistakes, but it clearly does. Unfortunately, people today place too much faith in computers. Machine learning is great, but don't worship it. Another aspect of the HAL 9000 computer portrayed in the film was actually realistic in the sense of what artificially intelligent computer systems can actually do in the real world, and what they might actually be used for.

The system in the movie detects a coming fault in a communications device. In the movie it turns out to be in error, but the point is many machine learning systems are being developed that will hopefully detect faults in electronics and machines before humans become aware of them.

We don't want to get too carried away with science fiction stories, but the analogies and interpretations of what is possible are interesting to consider.

It turns out that hype won the day, and after a few decades of pursuing the holy grail of artificial intelligence, in effect creating a computer system that worked like a human brain, computer scientists began to change direction.

They turned more attention to machine learning, which is something that can be thought of as using humanlike intelligence but applied to a very narrowly tailored task.

Something that was missing, however, was data.

Big Data and Machine Learning

In order to learn something, a system that is capable of machine learning needs to be exposed to a lot of data. Going back several decades, computers didn't have access to all that much data, in comparison to what they can access today. Computers were slow and quite awkward. Most data at that time was stored on paper, and so it was not readily accessed by computer systems. There was also far less of it. Of course, companies and large businesses, along with governments have always collected as much data as they could, but when you don't have that much data and it's mostly in the form of paper records, then you don't have much data that is useful to a machine learning computer system.

The first databases were invented in the late 1960s. A database is not really what we think of when considering the relationship between data and machine learning, although it could be in some circumstances. Databases collect very organized information.

To understand the difference, think about a collection of Facebook posts, versus a record of someone registering to enroll at a university. The collection of Facebook posts is going to be disorganized and messy. It is going to have data of different types, such as photos, videos, links, and text. It's going to be pretty well unclassified, maybe only marked by who posted it and the date.

In contrast, when you say database you should think completely organized and restricted data. A database is composed of individual records, each record containing the same data fields.

At a university, students when enrolled might enter their name, social security or ID number, address, and so on. All of these records are stored in the same format, together in one big file. The file can then be "queried" to return records that we ask for. For example, we could have it return records for everyone in the Freshman class.

Relational databases allow you to cross reference information and bring it together in a query. Following our example, you could have a separate database that had the courses each student was taking. This could be stored in a separate database from the basic information of each student, but it could be cross referenced using a field as a student ID.

Tools were developed to help bring data together from different databases. IBM, a company that always seems to figure large in many developments in computer science, developed the first structured query language or SQL, that could be used to do tasks like this. Once data could be pulled together, it could be analyzed or used to do things like print out reports for human operators. As computers became more ubiquitous, companies and government agencies began collecting more and more data. But it wasn't until the late 1990s that the amount of data and types of data began to explode. There were two developments that led to these changes. The first was the invention of the internet. The second was the development of ever improving and lower cost computer storage capacity. The development and commercialization of the internet meant that over a very short time period, nearly everyone was getting "online". Businesses moved fast to get online with websites. Those that didn't fall behind, and many ended up going out of business. But that isn't what's important for our purposes.

The key here is that once people got online, they were leaving data trails all over the place. This kind of data collection was increasing in the offline world as well, as computing power started to grow. For example, grocery stores started offering supposed discount and membership cards, that really functioned to track what people were buying, so that the companies could make customized offers to customers, and so they could adjust their marketing plans and so forth.

The internet also brought the concept of cloud computing to the forefront. Rather than having a single computer, or a network of computers in one office, the internet offered the possibility of harnessing the power of multiple computers linked together both for information processing and doing calculations and also for simple data storage.

A third development, the continual decline in the costs of storage components of computer systems along with increased capacity had a large impact in this area. Soon, more and more data was being collected. Large companies like Google, and eventually Facebook, also started collecting large amounts of data on people's behavior.

This is where machine learning hits the road. For the first time, the amounts of data that machine learning systems needed to be able to perform real world tasks, not just do things like playing checkers, became possible.
Machine learning systems are trained on data sets, and now businesses (and governments) had data of all kinds to train machine learning systems to do many different tasks.

Goals and Applications of Machine Learning

Machine learning is something that can be applied whenever there is a useful pattern in any large data set. In many cases, it is not known what patterns exist before the data has been fed to a machine learning system. This is because human beings are not able to see the underlying pattern in large data sets, but computers are well suited to finding them. The types of patterns are not limited in any way. For example, a machine learning system can be used to detect hacking attempts on a computer network. It can be trained for network security by feeding the system past data that includes previous hacking attempts.

In another case, a machine learning system can be used to develop facial recognition technology. The system can be presented with large numbers of photographs that contain faces, so that it can learn to spot faces, and to associate a given face with a particular individual.

Now let's consider another application of machine learning, which is completely different from the other two we've looked at so far. Machine learning can be used to approve or disapprove a loan application. During the training phase, the system will be exposed to a large number of previous loan applications and the ultimate results. In other words, did the borrower pay the loan off early or default on the loan? During the exposure to all the data, the system will learn what characteristics or combinations of characteristics best predict whether or not a given applicant is going to default on a loan. This is all done without human input, and so the machine may find patterns in the data that human observers missed and never suspected were there. The fact is that human minds are not very good at being able to analyze large data sets, and some would probably argue that we can't do it at all.

One of the earliest applications of machine learning was in the detection of email spam. This is a good example to look at, because it illustrates a particular type of problem that machine learning systems are good at solving. Determining whether or not an email is spam or not is something that can be framed as a classification problem. In other words, you take each email, examine it, and classify it as spam or not spam. This is not something that can be taken to be absolute, and detecting all spam messages can be tricky.

Fraud detection with credit and debit cards is yet another application of machine learning. By studying past data, the system can learn to detect patterns in usage that indicate that the card is being used in a fraudulent manner. In many cases, the patterns that are detected are going to be things that human observers are completely unaware of, or wouldn't associate with fraud detection even if they knew the patterns existed.

So, we see that machine learning can be applied in virtually any situation where there is a large amount of data available, and there are patterns in the data that can be used for the purposes of detection or prediction. Machine learning is quite general, able to learn anything from playing chess to spotting fuel waste for an airline like Southwest.

This is not the artificial intelligence that was once imagined by science fiction writers in the 1960s or 1970s, but it does have many characteristics of human learning. The first is that it's quite general. The second is that it will perform better, the more data that it is exposed to.

Now let's consider the goals of machine learning. The central goal of machine learning is to develop general purpose algorithms that can solve problems using intelligence and learning. Obviously one important goal of machine learning is to increase productivity. This is true whether or not the user of the system is a business, a military branch, or a government agency.

The second goal is to replace human labor with better machine labor. Of course, this has been a goal of technology ever since the industrial revolution started, and it continues to be an important goal today. However, the way that this is being done in the case of machine learning is a little bit different. The first thing is using machine learning to perform tasks that require a level of attention and focus that human beings are not able to provide. Even when humans are excellent workers who will provide maximum focus, a human suffers from many flaws, like fatigue, and the ability to be distracted. Also, the amount of information that a human observer can pay attention to at any given time is very limited.

Consider a machine learning system instead–focus is never an issue. A computer system is able to generate laser-like focus in a way that a human being never could. Second, it is able to analyze and sample a far larger data set, and of course it will never be subject to fatigue and it's not going to need restroom breaks or lunch.

One application–in a general sense–that is being used in many businesses today is using machine learning to spot waste. Several large corporations have already had great success with this. We've already mentioned one, Southwest Airlines famously used machine learning to analyze the activity of airlines on the tarmac, and they found a great deal of waste in terms of time and fuel was spent by planes idling on the tarmac. UPS has also used machine learning to spot wasteful driving routes that cost the company time and money, at the expense of having thousands of trucks waste gallons of fuel. Machine learning can also be applied to find out what employees are doing and how they can better use their time.

Benefits of Machine Learning

There are a large number of benefits for businesses that use machine learning. We can summarize a few of them here:

- Machine learning can easily find patterns in any underlying data set.

- Systems based on machine learning get better with experience. The more data they see, the better they are going to get.

- Machine learning is quite general, and can be applied to nearly any application, from detecting hacking attempts on a computer network to picking winning stocks.

- Machine learning systems can handle multidimensional problems that would overwhelm human observers.

- Once a system has gone through the learning phase, further human intervention is not required. This is a true system that uses automation.

- Machine learning can be applied across a broad spectrum, and it can be used to solve nearly any problem that a business may encounter.

How Machine Learning Works

Machine learning begins with a human guide in the form of a data scientist. A problem has to be identified that a machine learning algorithm can be used to solve it. In order for the process to work, there must be a significant amount of data that can be used to train the system before it is deployed in the real world. There are two basic ways that machine learning can proceed, and we will discuss these in detail in the next chapter. They are called supervised and unsupervised learning.

In the training phase, the data scientist will select appropriate training data, and expose the system to the data. As the system is exposed to data, it will modify itself in order to become more accurate. This phase is a crucial part of a development with the system, and the data scientist must choose the right data set for the problem at hand. In other words, the impression that human beings are not involved at all is completely false. Human beings are involved in choosing and framing the problem, and in choosing the right training data. The human being is also involved in the process of evaluating the performance of the system.

As we will see, there are tradeoffs that must be made that have large implications for the viability of the system. If the data scientists that are working on the problem are not careful and correct, to the best of their abilities, in interpreting the results produced by the system, a dysfunctional system can be deployed that will err when attempting to do its job.

The training phase may have several iterations, depending on how the results turn out.

Once the system is deployed, it will more or less operate in an autonomous fashion, but data scientists that are involved in this work should be continually evaluating the performance of the system. At some point, the system may need to be replaced or it may need to be subjected to more training, if it is not producing the kinds of results that are accepted.

Steps in Machine Learning

The data scientist must follow a certain procedure in order to implement machine learning. In the following chapters we will learn the two different approaches that are used in "training" the system. Machine learning involves artificial intelligence, and so any system that has artificial intelligence is just like a human being, in that the system needs to learn it's skill before it goes out into the real world. It is up to the data scientist to provide the training that the system needs. In this section we are going to outline the general steps that are needed, in the following two chapters we will discuss the specific methods used.

Define the Problem

Each step in the machine learning paradigm is critical. If you make a mistake early on, this is going to make the entire enterprise fall flat. When you say artificial intelligence, while you get the impression that there is an all-powerful computer, like the HAL 9000 system from 2001, the reality is a little more down to earth. It is true that there is not a specific, line by line set of instructions written in code by human engineers that tell the computer what to do, and once a machine learning system is deployed people might not really understand how it's working. Nonetheless, there is a lot of direct human involvement in the process. And given our propensity to make mistakes, it's important to be careful at each step along the way. Think of yourself as a teacher guiding a child so that they learn a new skill.

The first step is having a clear definition of the problem that you are facing. The end goal must be in mind, so you must know what you expect the machine learning system to do when it is up and running.

Gather and Prepare Data

The second step is to gather the data that is necessary to use in order to train the system. If you define the problem but there is little or no data that can be used to train it, then this procedure is not going to work.

Machine learning must have enough data so that the system can determine patterns and relationships in the data that will allow it to make predictions and classifications in the real world. The assumption is going to be that enough data of the right type has been collected. But simply having the data is not enough. As we will see, if you simply feed the system raw data, this can create problems for a number of reasons. So you will have to take a look at the data and apply some human judgment to it. Think of data as consisting of a large number of fields or properties. Are all of the properties relevant to the problem at hand?

In many cases, a machine learning system is going to find relationships among different properties that do have a predictive value that humans will miss–so there is a balancing act between cutting down the data versus removing something that might be very important, even though it doesn't seem relevant to the human operator.
Nonetheless, you don't want to have too much information in the data set that can make it impossible to learn.
So, you might have to discard some data to reduce the complexity of the problem, if this is possible. We will discuss more details about this in later chapters.

Choose the Style of Learning

We will see in the next few chapters that there are different methods of learning. These are going to be based on the nature of the problem and the type of data that you have. This is an easy step in the process, since that will dictate the style of learning used. The main types of learning are supervised learning, unsupervised learning, semi-supervised learning, and representational learning. We will learn what types of problems each type of learning is suitable for and how the structure of the input data differs in the next couple of chapters.

Select the Most Appropriate Algorithm

Once you have settled on whether or not the data and the problem you are solving is best suited for supervised or unsupervised learning, then you need to decide which algorithm to use. Certain situations might dictate whether one algorithm is better than another algorithm. Choosing the right algorithm might have an influence on the types of errors that you see in the results. This means that as someone who is using machine learning, understanding the main types of algorithms is going to be important.

Train and Test

Now at this point, everything is ready to go. The first step is to expose the system to the training data so that it can learn. Then you will test the system and evaluate.

Improve

When you evaluate the performance of the system with training and test data, the error will need to be quantified. If the error is not acceptable, adjustments may have to be made. As you would with regular coding, you can go through a cycle of more training and making adjustments to reduce errors. In some cases, you might have to scrap the system and start over, but one of the benefits of machine learning is that the system is adaptive. The more data it sees the better it learns. So, improvement may be possible by simply exposing the system to more training data.

Deploy

Once the system is working to the degree that has an acceptable level of error, then it is ready to be deployed.

Chapter 10: How Machine Learning is Applied in the Real World

It's one thing to talk about machine learning in the abstract. To get a better handle on machine learning, we also want to understand how it's being used in businesses and other large organizations today in order to perform useful functions. First, let's understand where machine learning fits into the overall framework of computer science and artificial intelligence.

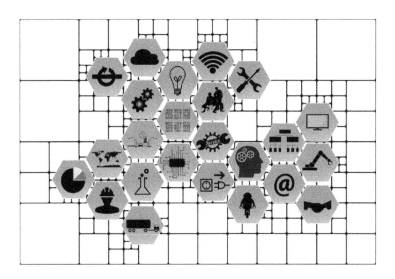

When Does Machine Learning Work?

When faced with a problem that is suitable for the deployment of a computer system, the first thing that you should ask about the problem is whether or not it is rigid and unchanging, or is this something that requires an adaptive system?

At first glance this seems like a simple question. For example, suppose that you were considering a ballistics program for the military. Ballistics follow the laws of physics. These are precisely known, and so it should be a simple matter to do calculations to get the accurate results that are desired. Hard coded computer programs can be used to predict how things will work in real situations. Indeed, as soon as Newton's laws were known in the 17th and 18th centuries, armies were using people to do the calculations by hand, and this helped to revolutionize warfare and military efficiency. Today it's done even better and faster using powerful computer technology.

But a recent example shows that there is often more to any situation than meets the eye. Consider an EKG, which can give a doctor a picture of the performance of the heart. An EKG is used to diagnose a heart attack, arrythmias, and many other problems. It's very narrowly focused, and patterns on the EKG are associated with specific conditions. Health professionals are trained to recognize those patterns, and they can study an EKG chart and determine which patients need medical intervention and which don't. This is as straightforward as the ballistics problem.

However, when artificially intelligent systems were developed using machine learning to study EKGs, it was found that they outperformed doctors by a significant margin. The machine learning systems that have been developed are able to predict which patients will die within a year with 85% accuracy. For comparison, doctors are able to make the same prediction with 65% to at most 80% accuracy.

The key here is the difference. When there are EKGs that look completely normal to the human eye–the machine learning system is able to determine that in fact, they are not normal. The engineers that designed the system can't explain it. They don't know why or how the machine learning system makes its predictions. But the way it works, generally speaking, is that the machine learning system is able to detect patterns in the data that human minds cannot detect.

This example serves to illustrate that adaptive learning can be used in nearly every situation. Even in ballistics, there may be many different factors that human engineers have not properly accounted for. Who knows what they are, it could be the humidity, wind, or other factors. The bet is that although line-by-line coded software works very well in deterministic situations, adaptive software that is not programmed and only trained with data will do better.

Complex and Adaptive

When there is any situation where experience–that is exposure to more data–can improve performance, machine learning is definitely called for. If the data is complex, this is another situation where machine learning can shine. Think about how the human mind can handle mathematical problems. Even two-dimensional problems in calculus and differential equations are difficult for most people, and even the smartest people struggle while learning it for the first time. It gets even more difficult when you move to three dimensions, and the more complexity that is added, the harder it is for people to digest. If you are looking at a data set, you are going to be facing the same situation. If we have a small data set of 20 items, each with 3 fields and an output, a human operator might be able to extract a relationship between the inputs and outputs. They could even do linear regression by hand or plug it into a simple program like Microsoft Excel. Even simply eyeballing the data can reveal the relationships.

But the more data you add to the problem, the less able a human operator is able to determine what the relationships are. The same problem with output but 20 inputs might make it very difficult. If there are no outputs, and you ask human operators to see if there are any patterns in the data, it might become virtually impossible. One way that we get around complexity in the real world is to program computers in the standard way. This helps humans get around many large data problems and solving problems that would involve tedious work. Consider weather prediction, early efforts at predicting the weather or modeling the climate were based on standard line-by-line coding, using the laws of physics and inputs believed to be important by the operator.

However, when there is a large amount of complexity in a problem, such as predicting the weather, this is a signal that machine learning is probably going to outperform any method by a wide margin. Think about climate modeling. Using conventional techniques, the scientists and programmers are going to make estimates of what factors (such as carbon dioxide level) are important.

But using machine learning, simply training the system on raw data, the system would probably detect patterns in the data that human observers don't even know are there, and it would probably build an even more accurate system that would be better at making future predictions. To summarize, when you have a problem that is adaptive and complex then it is well suited for machine learning. But there is a third component, and this is big data.

The Role of Big Data

Over the past two or three decades, there has been a quiet revolution in computing power that went unnoticed at first. Developments in technology made it possible to develop more storage capacity, and the costs of this storage capacity have continually dropped. This phenomenon combined with the internet to make it easy for organizations that are large and small to collect enormous amounts of information and store it. The concept of big data was born.

Big data is of course large amounts of data. However, experts characterize big data in four ways. Simply having a static set of large amounts of data is not useful unless you can quickly access it. Big data is characterized by the "four V's".

- *Volume*: Huge amounts of data are being created and stored by computer systems throughout the world.
- *Velocity*: The speed of data movement continues to increase. Speed of data means that computer systems can gather and analyze larger amounts of data more quickly.
- *Variety*: Big data is also characterized by collection methods from different sources. For example, a consumer profile can include data from a person's behavior while online, but it will also include mobile data from their smart phone, and data from wearable technology like smart watches.
- *Veracity*: The truthfulness of the data is important. Do business leaders trust the data they are using? If the data is erroneous, it's not going to be useful.

The key to focus on here is that big data plays a central role in machine learning. In fact, without adequate amounts of accurate (truthful) data that can be accessed quickly, machine learning wouldn't work. The basic fundamentals of machine learning were developed decades ago, but it really wasn't until we moved into the 21st century that the ability to collect and move data around caught up to what was known about machine learning. The arrival of big data is what turned machine learning from an academic curiosity into something real that could be deployed in the real world to get real results.

Where Does Machine Learning Fit In?

Now that we understand the relationship of machine learning to big data, let's see where machine learning fits in with other concepts in computer science. We begin with artificial intelligence. Artificial intelligence is the overarching concept that entails computer systems that can learn and get better with experience. Artificial intelligence can be characterized by the following general characteristics:

- The ability to learn from data.
- The ability to get better from experience.
- The ability to reason.
- It is completely general, as the human brain. So, it can learn anything and can learn multiple tasks.

Machine learning is a subset of artificial intelligence. Rather than being completely general and engaging in humanlike reasoning, machine learning is focused on a specific task.

There are four major areas of machine learning, and within each of these there are specialties:

- *Supervised learning*–good for predictions of future outputs.
- *Unsupervised learning*–good for classifying objects.
- *Reinforcement learning*–a type of learning that encourages ideal behavior by giving rewards.
- *Deep learning*–A computer system that attempts to mimic the human brain using a neural network. It can be trained to perform a specific task.

Some Applications of Machine Learning

We have touched on a few ways that machine learning is used in the real world. To get a better feel for machine learning and how it's applied, let's go through some of the most impactful ways that it is being used.

Crimes and Criminal Activity

When you think about machine learning, think patterns. One very practical use of machine learning is exposing a system to past data from criminal activity.

This data can contain many different fields or features. They could include:

- Type of crime committed.
- Location of the crime.
- Time of day.
- Information about the perpetrator or perpetrators.
- Information about the victim.
- Weapons used.
- Day of the week and day of the month.
- Year when the crime occurred.

By studying the data and looking for hidden patterns, a machine learning system can be built to predict the incidents of future crimes. This doesn't mean that it is going to be able to predict a specific crime "there will be a robbery at 615 main street at 6 PM", but rather it will predict overall patterns of criminal activity.

This activity might vary in ways that even experienced law enforcement officers are unable to predict–reflect back on the EKG example. How can this help in the real world? It can help law enforcement agencies deploy resources in a more efficient manner. Even if they don't understand why a given system is making the predictions it's making, they can benefit by moving more law enforcement resources into areas that the system is telling them are going to experience more criminal activity, on the days and at the times when those resources are needed the most. This can help police and emergency personnel respond to crimes more rapidly, and it can also help deter crime with a greater police presence.

Hospital Staffing

Hospital staffing suffers from a similar problem. Human managers attempt to guess when most doctors and nurses are needed and where they should be deployed. While these estimates are reasonably accurate, improvements can be made by deploying a system that uses machine learning. Again, think back to the EKG example–a doctor is pretty good, giving results with 65-80% accuracy. But the machine learning system is even better with 85%, picking out situations the doctors miss. That kind of difference can be a large matter of life or death when it comes to efficiently allocate staff in a large hospital.

To put together systems of this type, large medical organizations tracked the locations and movements of nurses. This allowed them to provide input data to the system, which was able to identify areas of waste. As a simple example, it might have discovered that a large number of nurses were idle on the 7th floor, while there were not enough nurses in a different ward of the hospital, and so patients there were not getting needed attention, and some may have died as a result.

The Lost Customer Problem

For a business, a loyal customer is worth their weight in gold–or far more. A loyal customer is one that is going to return to make repeated purchases. Or even better, they will subscribe. What do you think is more valuable to companies like Verizon and T-Mobile, selling you the phone, or the fact that you sign up for possibly years of regular monthly payments?

Since loyal customers keep business profitable, learning why customers leave is very important. Even just a decade ago, this had to be done using guesswork. But now, vast sums of data have been collected on customers by large corporations. Preventing their customers from switching to a different company is something they are heavily focused on, and machine learning is enabling them to look for patterns in the data that can help them identify why a customer leaves, and even predict when a customer is about to leave.

This data can include basic demographics, usage patterns, attempts to contact customer support, and so on. The first step where machine learning can be used is that customers that have switched to another company can be identified, and then the system can learn what underlying patterns there are that would enable it to predict what customers are going to leave in the future.

Another way that this data can be used, is to study retention efforts. Once a customer is identified that is likely to leave, perhaps they can be offered a special deal. For example, a cell phone company could offer a large discount on a new phone, if they sign up for another two year contract. Or they could offer them free minutes or unlimited data.

Over time, more data is going to be collected. Machine learning can be applied again, this time to determine which methods work the best and what patterns exist–in other words what method works best for what customers. Maybe you will find that customers of different ages, genders, or living in different locations, or working at different types of jobs, will respond in different ways to inducements offered to retain the customer. This type of analysis will allow the company to tailor it's responses to each additional customer, improving the odds that they can keep the customer. The customers themselves will be happier, feeling that the company is responsible for their personal needs. The data will also help the company anticipate future market changes and help them adapt using predictive analytics.

Robotics

Using machine learning to develop better and more capable robotics is a huge area of inquiry. Robotics started out simple, performing rote tasks that don't require a huge amount of thought. For example, in the 1980s robotics were introduced on assembly lines to put in a screw or do some other task. The problem then was simple, the robot would perform a small number of exact, rote tasks that could be pre-programmed.

Now robotics are becoming more sophisticated, using cognitive systems to perform many tasks that are tedious but were once thought to be something that only human beings could do. For example, recently robots have been developed that can work as fast food cooks. This is going to have major implications for unskilled labor, because there are two factors at play in the current environment. Activism is pushing up wages for hourly employees doing unskilled labor, while the costs of robotics that can perform the same tasks are dropping. Moreover, the abilities of the robots to perform these tasks continually improves. A breakeven point is going to be reached. That is the cost of buying and operating a robot will be less than the costs of hiring a human employee. The robot will never waver in efficiency, it won't require the payment of employment taxes, and it's never going to file a lawsuit or allege discrimination. From the employer's perspective, automation is going to be preferable and this trend probably can't be stopped.

Over the past year, many sophisticated robots have been revealed to the public. Boston Dynamics, for example, has built robots that can work in warehouses.

They are able to identify packages that need to be moved, pick them up, and then place them where they need to be. At the present time, the only thing preventing widespread adaptation of this type of technology is cost.

A working robot like this has to be able to interact with the environment that it is in, in addition to performing the required task. This means that a sophisticated computer system has to be in place in the robot that includes many machine learning systems. The machine learning systems will include movements required to perform the task, and the ability to avoid running into someone or another robot. Another form of artificial intelligence, computer vision, plays a significant role in the development of robotics, helping it to identify objects (and people) that are in the robot's environment. Since modern robotics is using machine learning, the ability of the robots to do their jobs and navigate the environments they are in will improve with time.

Virtual Assistants

One way that machine learning is having a direct impact on people right now is via personal assistants. Not only are these systems able to "think" in simple ways, look things up and follow instructions, but they are also able to understand language and engage in conversation. Think about the computer systems portrayed in Star Trek back in the 1960s– the users of the system would engage it using speech. Perhaps they were prescient or maybe the show actually directed where computer science research went, but today we have Alexa and Siri that basically work in the same way.

Of course, these systems are far from perfect, but they are improving with time, and the number of tasks and the complexity of the tasks they are assigned to do will increase.

Robo Advisors

One of the breakthroughs in machine learning is using machine learning systems to determine what stock trades to enter into in order to earn an investor profit. This amazing technology is called a robo-advisor, with a robot taking over the role of a financial advisor. Robo-advisors started out as tools used by traders looking to make lightning fast trades, but over time their use has expanded. If there is one place where there is big data, the stock market certainly qualifies. Using the data of past trends in stock prices under different conditions, machine learning systems can learn how to invest and trade stocks and other financial securities like options in order to make profits, no matter what your goals are. The systems allow users to specify what their investment or trading goals are, and then the robo-advisor will make the trades that it determines will help the investor reach those goals.
Robo-advisors are also becoming popular on the Forex market, where traders are engaged in making fast, short-term trades in order to make profits.

As time goes on, there is no question that robo-advisors are going to see an increasingly prominent role in the financial markets, and declining costs will help to make these tools available to more people.

Underwriting

One of the biggest components of financial work is underwriting for insurance and loans. Increasingly, large companies that use underwriting are relying on systems built around machine learning, rather than using human beings. One thing that is driving this trend is the fact that over the decades, companies have gathered enormous amounts of data on applicants that can be used by machine learning systems to predict the outcome of giving someone a loan or life insurance. The data will include information like age, gender, occupation, income, and so forth. Again, while it might seem "obvious" what factors will determine who is a good risk and who isn't, the EKG example showed us that significant improvements could be made using machine learning, which will detect patterns in the data that human observers are not aware of. By using these types of systems to approve loans and engage in other financial decisions, companies can reduce the risk of default and other problems.

Customer Service

Many large companies are increasingly using machine learning as the basis of their frontline customer service. Admittedly, this is working with mixed results, and it is obvious there is more work to be done. One way that these types of systems are being used is through the use of chatbots. While these systems have not been brought anywhere near perfection, they are saving companies money by having an automated system in place to solve the most basic problems that arise in customer and technical support.

With these systems in place, a great deal of low-skilled human labor can be eliminated, and human workers can be reserved to deal with more extensive problems and consumer inquiries. Chat bots can be used for bill paying and other rote activities as well. With time, the performance of these systems is sure to improve.

Real Time Pricing

One of the biggest problems anyone in business faces is setting the right price for their product or service. Large amounts of data have to be analyzed in order to make the right decision, and by the time a human manager could make the decision, market conditions may have changed. Machine learning gives companies an edge they didn't have before, by giving them the ability to use dynamic pricing models. A machine learning system can look at real data collected over long time periods, and determine optimal prices that will help companies deal with the tradeoffs of quantity sold versus profit earned, and then incorporate that into dealing with any issues related to competition and shifting market conditions. Machine learning can then respond in real time, lowering prices when demand drops to stimulate sales, or responding to a price cut by a competitor.

Product Recommendations

Machine learning systems on the internet are constantly tracking our behavior, and they attempt to learn from our behavior to predict what we are going to want to buy. These systems are another example of a system that is not perfect, they cannot tell if you are genuinely interested in something or looking something up for a friend, or looking at something you would never buy out of curiosity. Many people find them annoying and consider this an invasion of privacy, but one thing that we can be assured of is that over time the systems will improve dramatically as they continually learn from gathering huge amounts of data.

We can expect that in the coming years these types of systems will be able to avoid the false positives that many people find annoying. The privacy issue is probably the big unknown here, if the kind of tracking that is necessary for these systems ever gets banned or regulated, they might not be in use at all in the future. The rub here is that data sharing between the big tech companies is necessary for these systems to work.

Google collects data on people searching the internet, and companies like Amazon are also tracking searches on their sites, while Facebook is tracking what you look at and like. Then all these data are shared between the companies so that advertisers can target specific and appropriate customers.

Self-Driving Cars

Multiple machine learning systems are being integrated into self-driving cars, creating one of the most sophisticated technologies ever devised. Although driving can be thought of as a relatively trivial skill for a human being to learn, it involves the integration of many different cognitive skills, including vision, interpretation, signs recognition, object recognition, following the road, avoiding collisions and so forth. While driving split-second decisions are often essential for safety, and the hope is that self-driving cars will be able to make those decisions better than a human being can.

Using machine learning, and gathering data by having test cars out on the road, remarkable progress has been made in a few short years. How far this technology is going to go is uncertain. Due to many thorny issues that are involved including liability questions and personal preferences, the self-driving capability may be limited to a role as an optional or supportive feature.

Some people have visions of self-driving technology completely revolutionizing transportation, including the use of self-driving trucks for long-haul transport, but it is hard to imagine the freeways packed with self-driving semi-trucks. However, you can at least see the possibilities of a self-driving transport system and robots that would load and unload the trucks, completely automating logistics in the transportation industry.

Video Recommendations

Sites like YouTube and streaming services such as Netflix are using machine learning to help users navigate the world of online video. Every time you use one of these sites, your behaviors are collected, stored, and analyzed. This data includes everything from the type of videos you watch, to whether or not you pause or rewind, or whether you leave the video early. This information is then used to offer you a set of recommended videos or programs. The recommendations are dynamic, so if your behavior changes, you will see your recommendations change as well.

Of course, this is another area where the systems are not perfect. The human mind is as mysterious if not more so than machine learning, and someone who has a long history of watching World War 2 documentaries might suddenly feel an urge to watch a comedy, and no machine learning system in existence today is going to be able to detect that.

Of course, if you start showing patterns, say wanting to watch a comedy after having watched a certain number of war documentaries, then the system will be able to learn from that and show you comedies you might want to watch at the appropriate times. But what these systems cannot do in most cases, is predict the unexpected when it comes to these specific applications.

Fraud Detection

We've talked about machine learning for fraud detection involving credit card theft, but it can be applied and is being used in other applications as well. For example, identity theft is something that can be rooted out using machine learning. Another area where machine learning is proving useful is with rooting out fraud in loan applications and even on tax returns. Recall that in the case of credit or debit card theft, certain anomalous behavior is going to be observed by the system. In the same way, the system can use clustering methods to spot anomalies when it comes to loan applications, filing of insurance claims, or the filing of a tax return.

Of course, an anomaly is not a guarantee that fraud has occurred. But what can be done at that point, is when the system detects an anomaly it can be passed on to human operators who can investigate the situation. This saves a lot of labor at a company, since human resources can be deployed for more in-depth investigation and critical decision making, rather than having to deploy people to do the tedious task of trying to identify the anomalies in the first place, and more than likely missing anomalies that the computer systems will detect. Spotting anomalies is something that is particularly susceptible to human flaws such as fatigue and inability to maintain the required level of focus for long time periods. The large amounts of data that are collected by large companies and organizations like the IRS also make this problematic for human operators.

Conventional computing is also not very good at this, because conventional computer systems would not be able to anticipate situations that are invisible to human operators.

Another factor to consider is that bad actors are always changing their approach, and so learning the new ways of committing fraud is something that a system must be capable of doing. Of course machine learning systems are ideal in those circumstances.

Drug Discovery

The development of new drugs can be massively increased and improved with all the data that is being collected in the medical and pharmaceutical fields. Data on genetics, illness patterns, and so forth can be fed to machine learning systems, which can then evaluate large numbers of possible pathways to save pharmaceutical companies a great deal of time and help them to avoid blind alleys. One of the biggest problems that come about when designing new drugs is many of them are going to prove ineffective. Machine learning systems are able to reduce the probability that a drug is not going to work.

Another major advantage is that machine learning systems can combine data on DNA with other information to help design medications that can be laser targeted to individuals. Because of the particular genetic makeup of different individuals, some drugs are going to work better for one person, but not for another. By using machine learning, companies can develop new drugs that can be targeted for specific genetic markers. Another way that machine learning is being used in the pharmaceutical industry is to find multi-drug combinations that will work better for specific individuals based on their genetic makeup when they have come down with a serious disease.

Safety is also an issue, people with certain genetic markers may be more susceptible to serious side effects, and machine learning can help to identify the proper treatments for this subset of patients.

Facial Recognition

One longtime area of research in the world of artificial intelligence that has been going on for decades is computer vision. At first, computer vision systems were quite simple and one of the things that plague computer vision is the enormous amount of data that is required for learning. But now in today's world, yesterday's liability is now an asset. The ability to quickly process large amounts of data has made it possible to take computer vision to a new level.

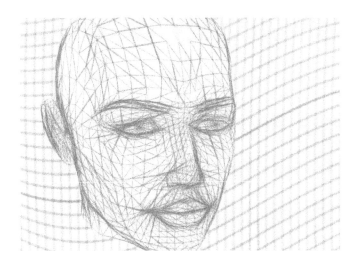

By exposing a machine learning system large numbers of images of faces, the systems have learned to take certain points on faces and use them to be able to identify individuals. We already see many applications of this machine learning technology. For example, Facebook uses facial recognition technology to identify individuals in any image that a user uploads, and people can be automatically "tagged" if they appear in an image. The error rate for this is surprisingly low.

The second application of this technology will be familiar to many readers. Apple introduced facial recognition technology with the iPhone X, and used it as a way to unlock the phones. It is probably going to be the case that facial recognition technology will find wider applications when it comes to security. For example, you could deny access to unauthorized users when they try and enter a building that is secured, whether it is an office or at home. Facial recognition is also being used in public by authorities as well. The systems are able to go through large amounts of data very quickly, enabling the development of real-time facial recognition that can pick people out of a crowd.

This technology can be used in positive or negative ways of course. Oppressive governments can use it to track people and determine where you are at any given time, but it can also be used to spot known terrorists in a crowd, and help law enforcement respond quickly to an event before it gets out of control. It is also being used for a government issued ID cards, so that people don't have to routinely get new drivers licenses or other documents.

As we age, the visual appearance of our face changes, but certain key characteristics of the face are constant (in most circumstances) and can be quickly analyzed by technology to identify an individual. So you get one photograph on a license that is good for all time unless you have had a disfiguring accident.

Types of Data

In addition to learning the wide range of applications that are suitable for machine learning, if you are going to be involved in this field you need to have a solid grasp on the types of data that are used.

Structured Data

Many businesses and large organizations collect large amounts of structured data, and they have been doing so for many decades. Structured data is information that is organized into particular formats. The classic example of structured data is a relational database. It has various fields that characterize a record in the database, which can be indexed in different fields for the purposes of sorting, searching, and retrieving subsets of the data. Structured data can also take many other different forms, as long as it is collected and organized.

For example, a grocery store can collect point of sale data, when customers check out.

This data can be arranged in a databased, identifying the customer through a so-called loyalty or discount card, and then combining that information with their purchasing habits in order to drive targeted marketing. Certain types of medical devices and other sensors can also be used to collect structured data. For example, you could collect the oxygen level of a patient in a hospital at different time intervals, and this information can be recorded permanently in a computer system with identifying information of the patient. Another type of structured data that most people are familiar with is a spreadsheet. Structured data plays an important role in business intelligence, and it can often be extracted and presented visually in the form of charts and graphs, to help management make important data driven decisions.

Unstructured Data

The fact is that most data is actually unstructured data. When we have unstructured data, there is not a specific format and it may not be amenable to organizational structures like spreadsheets or relational databases. It might also have many mixed media types.

For example, the Facebook postings of a given user can serve as a representation of unstructured data. Although a posting can be classified as to the user, date, and time of the posting, there are many different types of information in the posting such as images, video, text, and hyperlinks. The data in an image or video is something that is not suitable for a relational database, and hence it is unstructured.

Another type of unstructured data that large organizations collect is data related to internal operations. This includes recorded phone calls, memos, emails, and images among other things. Companies often collect reams of this data but have no idea how to use it, organize it, or access it. Unstructured data is definitely amenable to use with machine learning. There are many ways that the internal data of a company can be used, for example the company could determine which employees are spending a lot of time in the office idle (that is, not engaged in work related activities). The unstructured data that a company collects could also be used to reorganize teams or move people from one department to another. The company can find out who is collaborating with whom, and then use that information to move employees around to better facilitate those communications, or make changes if the management feels that they are not communicating with team members they should be communicating with.

Text documents can be analyzed by machine learning programs to detect patterns that management is not even aware of, and then this information could be used to reorganize company operations to increase efficiency and productivity.

There are many types of unstructured data, but to give you an idea of what might constitute unstructured data, let's quickly give an overview:

- *Photo and video*: Images and videos of all types can constitute unstructured data. Consider the video surveillance footage collected by many businesses. That is unstructured data.

- *Traffic data*: One area that is now routinely tackled by machine learning is traffic patterns. Machine learning systems can help people by analyzing the unstructured data that is gathered on traffic patterns in busy locations, and this can then be used to suggest alternative routes.

- *Mobile data*: Unfortunately, depending on your point of view, the more dependent we become on our smart phones, the more large companies (and government agencies in some situations) are able to monitor our behavior. Your location data, usage data of apps and text messages, all constitute unstructured data that can be analyzed by machine learning systems to find hidden patterns that can be used for predictive purposes or classification.

- *Social media data*: Any data from your usage of Facebook, Twitter, Instagram, LinkedIn or other social media sites are a treasure trove of unstructured data that can be used to predict what products you are interested in or your future behaviors.

- *Satellite information*: Satellite imaging is a good example of unstructured data.

- *Transcripts of phone calls*: Whether it's an internal phone call between members of your sales staff or a transcript of a technical support call, the unstructured data in that transcript can contain a great deal of information that could be useful to the organization.

It is estimated that at least 80% of recorded information is unstructured data that is not contained in relational databases or other formats. Unstructured data is being generated constantly, every second of every day. By analyzing and utilizing unstructured data, companies can significantly improve competitiveness, efficiency, and productivity. If you aren't using unstructured data, that means that you are leaving a lot of important information on the table. Unstructured data can reveal trends before people even realize they are happening. For example, a company could discover that a trend is building in people abandoning a specific product, or the seemingly random posts on Twitter and Facebook might reveal a trend that was happening at large in society that is under the radar of most people.

Summary

The examples discussed in this chapter serve to illustrate the wide range of problems that can be tackled using machine learning. As you can see from these examples, the applications are quite diverse. This diversity is possible because of the general nature of machine intelligence. A human being can learn to become a doctor, or a financial analyst. They can learn how to ride a motorcycle or how to play chess. This type of general intelligence that human beings possess has been the inspiration for the development of artificial intelligence. Any given machine learning system will be quite specific as to what it learns and does, and once it's trained on something, that is what it's going to do. But by combining several machine learning systems together, we can create an integrated system like a robot that can be used to perform multiple tasks.

Chapter 11: Supervised Learning

A machine learning system must be trained. This is done by presenting it with data.

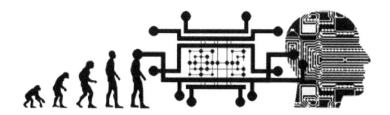

+

There are three ways that machine learning systems undergo training, or a learning phase. The two main methods that are used are known as supervised and unsupervised learning. A third method is available, which is called semi-supervised learning. In this chapter, we are going to learn the ways that these methods are used, the purpose of using them, and how they differ from one another. We will begin by considering supervised learning, since this is considered a bit more basic.

However, the application, rather than any thoughts about complexity, is going to be what determines the types of learning that are used.

Supervised Machine Learning

The term supervised or unsupervised refers to the training portion in the life of the machine learning system. The first main technique that is used is called supervised machine learning. This is most appropriate when you have a large data set that has clearly defined inputs and outputs. Another way to put this is that given a certain input set of data, we know what the output, or correct answer is. We say that the data in this case is labeled. This simply means that the various fields in the data are labeled as an input or an output.

Mathematically, we are considering a basic functional form in this case:

$Y = f(X)$

Here X is the input, and Y is the output, and f is an unknown functional relationship between the two. The point here is not to be thinking in terms of specific mathematical relations, but rather in terms of an abstract relationship that exists between the inputs and outputs. In some cases, there will be a precise functional relationship, but in many cases, we are not going to know what the relationship is, even though the computer system will "know" how the inputs and outputs are related. It will discover this relationship by detecting the hidden patterns that exist in the data that can be used to related inputs and outputs (and are probably unknown to the human observers). As a simple example, suppose that we were selling our own smart phone, and we wanted to find out who the ideal customer was.

For the sake of simplicity, suppose that our data only records the gender, age, and zip code of each customer of our phone service. We can then simply label each customer as a yes or a no as to whether or not they purchased the smart phone. Our input vector is going to be gender, age, and zip code, while the labeled output–which is given to the system as a part of supervised learning–is a marker as to whether or not the given customer purchased the phone.

Prior to doing the exercise, we may not have any idea about what characteristics are most important in determining whether or not a given customer is likely to purchase the phone or not, but the system might determine that females aged 30-45 are most likely to purchase the phone.
With this information in hand, we can then target a larger share of our advertising budget to this group.

The real world is complicated, and there are not going to be simple scalar relationships between the inputs and outputs, and they are not going to be simple scalar variables. Instead, the inputs and outputs are going to be in the form of vectors. A vector is a mathematical quantity that contains multiple elements. In the case of data that is used in machine learning, the vector will contain multiple fields of data. It is important to think in general terms, and so the data is not necessarily numerical in nature, although it could be. The supervised learning process is often likened to an elementary school class that is guided by a teacher.
For example, think about teaching children how to multiply two numbers together. This can be setup by thinking in terms of giving input vectors such as (2,2), (4,3) and (7,5), together with the known outputs (4), (12), and (35). This is an example of labeled data, where we have inputs, e.g. (4,3) and labeled outputs, e.g. (12).

In the same way, inputs and outputs are labeled for the computer system by the data scientist. Then the computer system goes through large amounts of data, in order to learn the patterns underlying the data and develop a relationship that can be used to predict outputs from future inputs. This is one of the core reasons that you would want to use supervised learning to train the system, in that you are hoping it will be able to predict future outputs. The output value during training is sometimes called the supervisory signal. A real-world example might be a data set of customers that got loans at a bank. Some of the customers will pay off the loan early. Others may default on the loan; some may keep making payments but be consistently late.

The goal in this case would be to look at the input data on each of these customers, and then try to determine the relationships that exist between the inputs and the outputs. In a complex real-world problem like this one, there are going to be many unexpected and hidden patterns in the underlying data that human observers could miss. Some of the relationships that exist between the inputs and the outputs will help the system make predictions of how a loan made to a new client will turn out based on the inputs that are provided.

Supervised learning can be thought of as a mapping process between input and output pairs. The purpose of training is to guide the system so that it can infer a relationship between the input and output vectors, and then that relationship can be used with any new data to predict the output. Of course, the training data is going to be limited in scope by necessity, and as a result the system is going to have to generalize to a certain degree in order to arrive at a relationship that can be applied to new data.

230

This process can result in problems, and there is an issue faced by all supervised learning systems that are called the bias-variance tradeoff. We will talk more about that later.

General Types of Supervised Machine Learning

Machine learning can be generally classified as either regression type learning, or classification. Generally speaking, in regression, the output variable may have continuous mathematical values.

In a classification problem, the labels are discrete and you can think of the input as being classified to belong to one group or another. Binary classification will assign a member to a group based on a 0 or a 1. In the earlier example where we considered whether a member of our phone service bought a phone or not, we could use binary classification, with buying the phone is a 1, and not buying the phone being a 0. However, classification problems can have more than two possible results.

The Process of Supervised Learning

The process of machine learning is going to be directed by a specialist on staff that is known as a data scientist. A data scientist is a professional that has training in multiple disciplines. At the very least, the data scientist should have training in computer science, especially in the fields of artificial intelligence and machine learning.

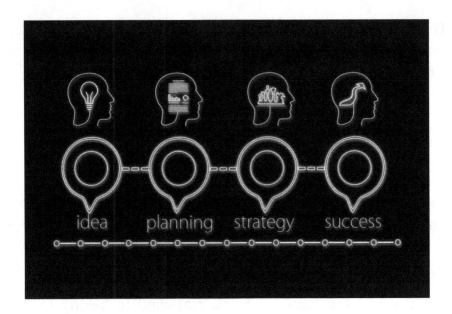

idea   planning   strategy   success

They should also have advanced training in statistics and probability, because these branches of mathematics have a large role to play whenever there are large data sets to be analyzed. Third, it is often desired that the data scientist has some business acumen, which will help them understand how the results of their work are going to be used by the organization and what the impact is going to be. There isn't really a formal definition of "data scientist" and until recently, there wasn't really any formal training or schooling for it.

This is a multidimensional field of expertise that has arisen in the real world do the coming together of several forces in the business and technological worlds.

The first skill that the data scientist must have is in the ability to select the best data sets available to use for learning, when faced with a specific problem.

Selecting the data can also mean refining the data, the data scientist may look at the fields of data and pare them down to a smaller number, that in the judgment of the human observer, seem more relevant to the problem at hand. As we will see, it is important to cut the number of fields down if there are a large number of them. Too many inputs for a system are going to make it harder for it to learn.

When we discuss artificial intelligence and machine learning, people often have a mystical view of it and might have the impression that the computer has an infinite capacity to examine data and learn. In fact, computer systems do not have an infinite capacity, even though they can examine and analyze much larger data sets than humans can. There may even be theoretical limits to the capacity of any intelligent system to do analysis and arrive at the correct result when there are too many inputs.

The problem of too many inputs causes issues because it becomes harder to determine the relationships between inputs and outputs. This is called the dimensionality problem. If there are too few dimensions, or fields representing an input to a problem, then there is not going to be enough information for the system to figure out the relationship between the inputs and the outputs.
On the other hand, if there are too many inputs or dimensions, then the system is going to be confused, and unable to find out what the true relationship between inputs and outputs are.

Again, you shouldn't be thinking of inputs and outputs as being strictly numerical in nature. For example, the problem at hand may be training a system in handwriting analysis. So, the input data might actually be images of handwriting.

Human experts working on the problem are going to choose data sets to use in training that they believe is representative of the real-world situation. Again, this is another aspect of the problem that is going to depend on the judgment of the data scientists that are setting up the training. It is another illustration of the fact that even though a machine learning system is not programmed, in the sense of having human operators write line by line instructions for the computer, it is nonetheless still heavily influenced by human decision making and judgment.

Feature Vectors

A feature is what it means in plain English. That is a feature is some measurable characteristic of a given input to a system. If the input is an image, some of the features that describe it could include the color, tint, brightness, and so forth of each pixel. If we are talking about a loan application, the features in question would be of a completely different nature. They could include credit score, bankruptcy (y/n), zip code, years of education, monthly income, and so forth.

Inputs are called feature vectors, because a feature vector is a representation of some object in the real world, that contains a set of features for that object.

For example, if we wanted to teach a system to recognize a truck or a car in a photograph, and determine the difference between the two, many aspects of the vehicle could be represented in the feature vector. It would be up to the data scientist to choose the features that they believe best represents the object of study.

Since some of the computer algorithms that are used in machine learning are numerical in nature, such as linear regression, a problem often has to be boiled down to numerical data. It is up to the data scientists to get the right representation in order to use the right algorithm, and they also have to be able to select the best features to represent a given object that is being studied. Obviously, this process is never going to be perfect, and at times there are going to be mistakes made.

Picking the Learning Algorithm

Once the problem has been broken down into input and output vectors, and the proper set of features has been selected, the data scientists must choose the best algorithm that can be used in order to represent the problem accurately. There are many different functions that are used. There are several different learning algorithms that are used. Choosing the algorithm that is used is another step in the process that is directed by a human being, and so this is another way that human observers and trainers are involved in influencing the final machine learning product. Let's review the type of algorithms that are used.

Linear Regression

Linear regression is one of the most popular algorithms that is used in machine learning. The purpose of using linear regression is to model a relationship between inputs and outputs that can then be used to predict future outputs. We will discuss linear regression in more detail in a future chapter.

Logistic Regression

Logistic regression, like linear regression, is a type of statistical modeling of some phenomenon. In this case, the output assumes a binary form. Therefore, we expect the output to be a type of yes/no, pass/fail, or alive/dead type of output.

Decision Trees

A decision tree is an algorithm that asks a series of questions at nodes about the characteristics of an item. This then follows along, leading to a path through different branches of a "tree" that will allow the system to arrive at a resulting answer or classification of a question being asked. For a real-world example where this could be used, think in terms of a diagnosis program.

A patient will present with a set of symptoms, and yes/no questions can then be posed about the symptoms and other characteristics to determine whether or not the patient has an illness and if so what kind of illness the patient is suffering from.

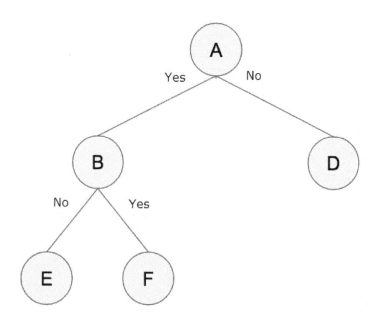

For example, you could use a decision tree in order to distinguish between allergies and a cold or flu. Does the patient have a fever? Is the patient experiencing body aches? And so on...the answer to one question will direct the system along a branchlike path in a tree to more questions. After several questions have been answered, eventually the conclusion is reached, in this case it would be a yes, the patient has allergies or yes, the patient has a cold/flu.

Naïve Bayes Classifier

In many cases, the purpose of machine learning will be to classify something. One common example of this that is used is spam email messaging, something we have touched on before. The point is that an email is classified as spam, or not spam. In recent years, email systems have become more sophisticated and they might classify email in more detail. So, we start with is the email spam or not spam, and if not spam, is it a personal email, a social email, or a promotion?

Of course, determining the difference between a promotion and spam is a more difficult problem, than determining whether an email is sent by a friend or whether it's a spam email. Nonetheless, systems like Gmail process such high volumes of email, and they have been doing it for large numbers of people over many years, that they are pretty good at sorting emails in this way (but of course, they still make many mistakes).

Bayesian classifiers use probability in order to classify inputs. Naïve Bayes means that naïve independence assumptions are made with regard to the input features in the problem. As the spam example illustrates, this type of algorithm can be used to label inputs. Supervised learning is suitable for this algorithm because the correct label would be the output of the system. So, the inputs to a system that was learning email via supervised learning would be the sending email address, the subject line used, the text of the email, and so forth. The possible outputs are the classifications of the email–is it from social media, is it spam, is it a personal email etc. These types of models use conditional probabilities, but the details are beyond the scope of this book.

Support Vector Machines

The next type of algorithm that is frequently used in supervised learning is called a support vector machine. Generally speaking, this type of algorithm is used when data can be classified as belonging to one data set or another. During training, the data inputs are provided, along with their classifications. This allows the system to build a model that represents the relationship between the input vectors and the classification. The beauty of this type of training is that although the human observer is somewhat involved, for example in selecting the inputs and outputs to present to the system, the human observer doesn't have to be involved in any way when it comes to determining the type of relationship that exists between the input and output data. Once the system has been trained, when it is presented with a new data point, it should be able to accurately classify the data as belonging to one classification or another.

K-Nearest Neighbor Algorithm

This type of algorithm can be used for classification or regression. In the case of supervised learning, regression is more likely to be important. The output in this case is some property of the object that is under study. The system will arrive at predicted outputs by observing the k-nearest neighbors, and then averaging the values of their outputs. Some mathematical function is used in order to precisely determine the "distance" between two different data points in a data set.

Conceptually, this is like a distance function between two points in space. The underlying assumption here is that when two data points in a set are close together, using the definition given in the distance function, they are going to have similar outputs. The neighbors can be weighted or unweighted. If they are unweighted, all neighbors that are used in the calculation are treated in the same manner, and so the predicted output is calculated using simple averaging techniques. If a weighted algorithm is used, then neighbors that are closer to the data point in question are given more weight than the neighbors that are more distant.

It is believed that generally speaking, the latter method is going to provide more accurate answers. However, which method you use in a given situation is going to be a matter of judgment. So once again, we have another point at which human judgment is involved in the process.

Neural Networks

A neural network is a model that is based on the way a brain functions. Hopefully, it is able to model a human brain, but as far as we know all brains work in basically the same manner. In an actual physical brain, there are neurons or nerve cells, that are able to hook up with or connect to other neurons. There is a cell body near the top of the cell, and several branches or dendrites extend out of the top of the cell body in a tree like formation. These each includes individual nodes that can connect to many other cells.

At the other end of the cell body, there is a long extension that resembles (at least conceptually) an electrical cable. This is called the axon. At the other end is more tree like dendrites, which are connected to other neurons. The sum total of inputs from the neurons connected to the front of the cell body will determine whether or not the neuron 'fires', which simply means that an electrical current will travel down the axon, leading to the release of chemicals out the other ends, that will help determine whether or not succeeding neurons fire or not.

Somehow, this process represents information processing, learning, and consciousness. While consciousness is not very well understood, the process of learning basically takes place as neurons form new networks among themselves, in order to represent information. Connections between neurons are strengthened or weakened, depending on experience and learning.

The goal of neural networks is to have a representation of this setup and the processes inside a computer.
Compared to a real brain, neural networks are quite primitive, nonetheless the general features of the process are there.

A nerve cell is represented by a "node", which is a computer function that might do some simple task. Actually, it is going to output a nonlinear function of some type of the inputs provided to the node, if communication has taken place. Inputs to a given node, from other nodes that are in the system, will be weighted. The weights will change as the system is exposed to new data. This is analogous to a physical neuron forming stronger or weaker connections to other neurons that are sending it input.

The weights will either be larger, strengthening the signal input from another node that is in another layer, or it will be smaller, weakening the signal.

An input layer of nodes will accept or take in information from the external world. There can be one or more hidden or intermediate layers. The first hidden layer is behind the input layer, and it will take inputs from the input layer. The outputs will serve as inputs for the next layer. If that is the last layer in a simple system, that layer will produce outputs for the external world. Alternatively, you can have multiple hidden layers.

As a neural network is exposed to data, the weights will adjust, changing the interconnections between the nodes or "neurons" in the system. A physical neuron will not fire unless a threshold is crossed with respect to electrostatic potential. In the same way, a node may have a threshold that must be reached before it will send an output signal to the neurons in the next layer.

Finishing the Process

We will talk about some of the more important learning algorithms in more detail in future chapters. It is important to recognize that you can't say one algorithm is better than any other algorithm. The judgment and experience of the data scientist must be used in order to determine the best algorithm to use in a given situation.

Once the algorithm has been selected, the data scientist will expose the system to the data. In some cases, the function used may be tuned by selecting the values of certain parameters that are used. These are called control parameters. The human observers will then evaluate the performance of the system, determining how well it performed. If it has not performed up to an acceptable level, then more training may be used, and there may be adjustments to control parameters to see if this will improve performance.

The Bias-Variance Tradeoff

One of the most important issues facing a data scientist and the use of supervised learning is the bias-variance tradeoff. These are errors in a prediction that result when a model is built. The goal when developing any computer model is to minimize errors. In the case of supervised learning, when you try to minimize variance errors, you will end up increasing bias errors. In turn, if you try to minimize bias error, you will increase error due to variance.

The key to success with supervised learning is simultaneously minimizing bias and variance. Of course, that means that we don't minimize either as much as we could minimize each in isolation. Therefore, a tradeoff is made, in order to reduce the overall total error. In other words, you will have to accept that there is going to be some level of error in both cases. When we are doing supervised learning, it is important to know what bias and variance refer to. Let's consider bias first.

243

Simply put, bias is the difference between the prediction of the model, and the correct answer, on average. If the model is very accurate with the training data, this means that the error between the prediction and the correct answer is going to be very small, but at the same time that also means that the model is going to be very biased toward the training data.

That could lead to errors in the real world, since the training data–to some extent–is not going to be representative of all the data that exists out there in the real world. This illustrates the importance of choosing representative training data. If the data scientist is able to choose training data that is highly representative of the data that the system is going to encounter in the real world when it is deployed, then there will not be as much bias.

Variance is the amount of spread, or variation in the data. Models with high variance will do very well on training data, but they will have problems with other data. The researchers developing the system will first present the system with training data, and then they will present it with test data.
When the system has a high bias, it will produce large errors with both the training and test data, and presumably also with any real-world data that it would encounter when deployed, if no modifications are made. If the system instead has high variance, it will have small errors with the training data, but will demonstrate high levels of error with the test data, and therefore with any real-world data that it encounters.

There are four situations that we can encounter, when considering bias and variance together:

- *Low Bias and Low Variance*: In this case, the model will be very accurate. It will give accurate results with training, test, and real-world data.
- *Low Bias, High Variance*: In this case, the data will overfit the training data. So, in training it will give very accurate results. But in testing or real-world situations, it will have high rates of error. It has overfitted the data used to train it.
- *High Bias, Low Variance*: In this case, the system is underfitting. Therefore, it is not going to be accurate, even with the training data.
- *High Bias, High Variance*: Here, we will be all over the map. The predictions of the model will not be accurate.

Underfitting and overfitting during training are things to look for when using supervised learning. Again, the data sets that are selected by the human observer are going to be important here. If the data set provided to train the system does not have enough data in it to accurately draw conclusions, underfitting can result. That means there will be high bias, but low variance. The model might be too simple to recognize the patterns in the data. Models that are particularly prone to underfitting include linear and logistic regression. Another way to look at it is that if the model is too simple, it can be prone to high bias and low variance. Remember that earlier, we mentioned the problem of dimensionality. In this case, that means we don't have enough parameters to correctly describe the problem.

Overfitting basically means that the system has fit the training data too closely. Any data set is going to have noise, or data that is intrinsically meaningless for the problem that is being studied. When the model overfits the data, it will fit the noise as well. So, it will perfectly fit (or nearly so) the training data set. But since it is being misled by the noise in the training data set, that means that in further testing on new data or in the real world, the model is going to be inaccurate. Decision trees are particularly prone to overfit the data. In this case, dimensionality may be a problem again. This time, we might have too many parameters. Ideally, you want to minimize both bias and variance as much as possible at the same time. This is done by minimizing the total error in the problem.

Matching Complexity to Bias and Variance

Any relationship between inputs and outputs is going to have its own level of complexity. If a problem is simple, that is the relationships between the features of the input vector and the output is simple, then a simple algorithm that has high bias and low variance might be able to learn the true relationship between inputs and outputs. Alternatively, the relationships between inputs and outputs may be highly complex. In that case, the algorithm needs to be flexible, and it will need a larger data set in order to learn the relationships between the inputs and the outputs. In that case, low bias and high variance algorithm will be better. These examples illustrate the problems that can arise and the amount of judgment that may be required in order to arrive at the best possible solution.

Dimensionality

The more features an input vector has, the more difficult the problem is to solve. Even if only a few features of the input vector are important to the output, if we don't know ahead of time which ones they are, this can create difficulties for the learning algorithm. The extra dimensions may serve to confuse the algorithm, by leading down the wrong direction. It may "detect" false relationships that don't actually exist. Mathematical procedures called dimensionality reduction may be used in order to try and eliminate features that are not important for determining the relationship between the input and output vectors in the problem. Alternatively, if not enough dimensions are provided as input, then the system may not be able to accurately predict future results, because not enough input features have been provided to the system.

Output Noise in Supervised Learning

Noise in the input data is one thing to worry about, and there is also a noise present in the output data that is used in supervised learning. There are many reasons that input data will have errors. In the course of real life, errors are going to be a natural occurrence. If human operators are recording or collecting data, they may make mistakes while recording results. In the normal course of operation, electronic devices may report erroneous results as well, for one reason or another.

As discussed earlier, this is why you want to avoid overfitting the training data, because you become attuned to the errors that are present in the training data set, that is not going to be characteristic of the data generally. One way to avoid this problem is to do some preprocessing of the data. In this instance, an effort can be made to reduce the noise in the data that is used for training before it is presented to the system.

Chapter 12: Unsupervised and Semi-Supervised Learning

In the last chapter, we introduced the first way that machine learning systems are trained. This was called supervised learning, and the training process in that case involves presenting the system with a set of data where the outputs are known and labeled ahead of time. Presenting the known outputs to the system in order to help it learn is how supervised learning works.

However, one of the main benefits of machine learning is that these types of systems are able to find hidden patterns in large data sets. This fact brings us to the next way that machine learning systems can be trained, and this procedure is known as unsupervised learning. In the process of unsupervised learning, the system is allowed to examine data and spot patterns within the data, drawing inferences about the data on its own. This is done without human direction and without any labeling of outputs. Since the outputs are not labeled (indeed, they may not be, and usually are not, even known), we can say that they are unlabeled. Often, the choice of using supervised or unsupervised learning will depend on the framing of the problem at hand, and the question as to whether you know what the outputs are. If the outputs are known then it makes sense to use supervised learning. But they may not be known, in which case unsupervised learning may be more appropriate.

Another type of learning attempts to mix the two. This will involve training on data sets using both supervised and unsupervised learning. In this case, we say that we are using semi-supervised learning. In this chapter, we will learn about unsupervised learning, and then wrap up the discussion by considering semi-supervised learning.

What is Unsupervised Learning?

In order to use regression, you need to be able to know what the output values are for the purposes of training, so that the data can be fit to some type of functional relationship. But with some data sets, we may not know what the outputs are, or we may be interested in using a large data set in order to determine if there are any hidden patterns or relationships in the data that we didn't even know existed. Clustering is one of the main methods used in unsupervised learning, so that the system can determine relationships between different members in the data set.

Clustering

In a large data set, you are going to find that the member objects can be grouped together in one or more ways. Consider an image. The pixels that make up the image can be classified by color. Then you could group together all yellow pixels, all orange pixels, all green pixels, all red pixels, all blue pixels, and all violet pixels in the image.

The key to clustering is grouping together data points that are more similar to each other than they are to other members in the data set. Algorithms are applied in order to do cluster analysis, clustering is the task that is to be completed, and not a specific way of doing the task.

When used with unsupervised machine learning, the machine is going to find the clusters on its own without human input. The human observers may not even know what clusters are present in the data, or they may only have a vague idea. A cluster is not even something that we can say what it is with any certainty. That will depend on the specific application, and in some cases, clusters may be defined with more or less rigor.

K-Means

K-means clustering gathers the data into k different clusters, determining which cluster a data point belongs to by how close it is to the mean of a given cluster. Often a human observer will look at the data to make an estimate of the number of clusters that should be used. The center or mean of each cluster is then calculated, and then as you sweep through the data, a distance function is used in order to find out which cluster the data point belongs to. This process is repeated in an iterative fashion, recomputing the mean values at each step.

Mean Shift Clustering

Mean shift clustering uses a window to sweep through the data. In this case, it begins by searching for areas with a high density of data points. The data is divided into different classes. As it sweeps through the data it attempts to find the center of each class. The center points are the mean of any data points that are inside the window. This algorithm will then sort the data into appropriate clusters.

While k-means clustering involves determining the number of clusters, in this case, the algorithm determines the number of clusters for you.

DBScan

This means Density Based Spatial Clustering of Applications with Noise. This is another density-based clustering algorithm. The algorithm picks an arbitrary starting point in a set of data. A distance function is used to determine a neighborhood about the point. The first step is to determine whether or not there are enough points in the neighborhood for analysis. If there are, then a cluster is formed. If there are not enough points in the neighborhood to form a cluster, then the point is determined to be noise.

Any data points that are within the distance that defines the neighborhood are determined to be members of the cluster. The algorithm will visit each of the points within the given neighborhood. Next, the algorithm will search outside the neighborhood to find an unvisited data point. It then repeats the process, determining if there are enough points in the neighborhood of the new data point to consider it valid and defining a new cluster, or if not, the point is labeled as noise and ignored.

There is no preset number of clusters, this is discovered by the algorithm. It is also able to determine if a data point is noise or not. Other clustering methods may not be able to do this. If the data has a high variance in the density of data points, the method may not be effective. The OPTICS method is an algorithm that was devised in order to address the density weakness problem of DBSCAN.

Hierarchical Clustering

This type of clustering can be either bottom-up or top-down. A bottom-up algorithm starts by considering every single data point to be a cluster. It then sweeps through the data, and then merges similar data points together to form new clusters. A distance function is used in order to determine whether or not two data points should be joined together to form a cluster. The sweeps through the system will continue, growing the number of points in each cluster. This type of clustering can be used to build a tree like structure. The leaves of the tree are the individual data points, and then going up each branch, you have each combination that was used to define a new cluster.

Anomaly Detection

One of the most useful ways that unsupervised learning can be used is with anomaly detection. Anomaly detection can be important in a wide variety of real-world circumstances. One of the most common ways that it is used is with the maintenance of security for computer networks. A machine learning system can examine past data that consists of attempts to access the network, and it can search for anomalies that are outside the statistically expected behavior of attempts at network access. When this occurs, then there is a certain degree of confidence that the access attempt is fraudulent.

When using unsupervised learning for anomaly detection, the central assumption that is made is that the majority of the collected data is completely normal. Therefore, the system will simply learn by searching for data that does not fit together with the rest of the data set. In other words, the system will search for outliers. It is then assumed that the outliers represent fraudulent activity.

Visualization

Systems trained with unsupervised learning can be used to determine hidden patterns in data, and then present the data in human readable form using visualization. In other words, the system will generate graphs and charts which will illustrate the relationships between features in the data.

Dimensionality Reduction

In the last chapter, the curse of dimensionality was mentioned several times. In some cases, the number of dimensions is excessive and having too many dimensions can make it difficult to determine the relationship between input and output variables difficult. Techniques of dimensionality reduction will attempt to cut down the number of features in the data set without losing important information. In the process of feature extraction, the system will merge together correlated features into one single feature.

By cutting down on the number of features, the time required to determine relationships between the data can be reduced, and it will make it more likely that a problem can be solved accurately. Principle component analysis and singular value decomposition are two techniques that can be used for dimensionality reduction.

Semi-Supervised Learning

In some situations, semi-supervised learning may be appropriate. This type of learning is a hybrid training strategy. Simply put, both supervised and unsupervised learning is used in this case. It has been shown that at least in some circumstances, the accuracy achieved with semi-supervised learning is superior to that seen with unsupervised learning alone. The key is to enhance unsupervised learning by training the system on a small dataset using supervised learning first. This can be thought of as a way to "prime" the system. Then the system can continue learning, but in the second phase of training, a larger data set is used for unsupervised learning.

Reinforcement Based Learning

Reinforcement learning is another strategy that can be used in machine learning. In this case, the system will have software agents that act within some kind of environment. A video game is an example of where this can be used.

Like unsupervised learning, this is another method that does not rely on using labeled input and output data pairs. In machine learning, reinforcement learning is centered on getting the machine to follow the best possible path in specific situations. The training is done by providing rewards. There will be a reinforcement agent that has to decide on its own how to perform various tasks. There are not any training datasets or labels used when building a system that is based on reinforcement learning.

A good way to understand reinforcement learning is to think in terms of a path through a maze. You can have a maze with obstacles that the agent must navigate around, and a reward somewhere in the maze that it must find. The agent will learn in the same way that a human being might learn, so you might imagine yourself in a corn maze trying to find a pot of gold. The agent will learn by trying different paths, and it learns solely through experience. When it tries a path and runs into an obstacle, then it will learn not to use that path again, and it will explore a different path instead. By trying out all possible paths and learning where the obstacles are, the agent will find its way to the reward. The agent can be encouraged to find the correct path by giving it rewards at various steps along the way.

Reinforcement learning is useful when there are multiple ways to solve a problem. A very simple problem like 2+2 has only one way to solve it, but in the real world, complex problems can often be solved in many different ways. In reinforcement learning, the agent will learn all the possible ways to solve the problem. When the agent is not performing in the right way, it can be punished and forced to start over. Every time that the agent is punished or rewarded, it will learn, and the next time it is sent back to the starting position, it will perform better so that it will be easier to reach its goal.

How Reinforcement Learning Compares to Supervised Learning

In supervised learning, we provide a set of data points and labeled answers to the system so that it can deduce the relationship there is between inputs and outputs. This is not done with reinforcement learning. Instead, the agent in reinforcement learning involves the agent making its own decisions, and then suffering the consequences of its own actions. This is how life is in reality, so it is a kind of model of real experience.

You can think of supervised learning as the kind of training that you would get in elementary school, while reinforcement training is the kind of learning that you experience in day to day life. When you start out now knowing very much, you are probably going to make many mistakes. But each time that you make a mistake, you learn not to pursue the actions that you took that led to the bad result. In the same way, the agent in reinforcement learning finds out which paths lead to punishment and which paths lead to rewarding.
After it learns this, then it no longer takes the bad paths, and it gets better at solving the task that it needs to solve.

Just like with real life, the behavior of the agent can be shaped using positive or negative enforcement, or some combination thereof. Positive reinforcement involves giving the agent a reward for making the right decision, while negative reinforcement involves giving the agent a punishment for making the wrong decision. If too much positive reinforcement is used, it can lead to diminishing returns over time. Maximal performance, however, is achieved by using positive reinforcement.

A minimal level of performance is achieved by training with negative reinforcement. A combination of the two can help the system learn without overwhelming it and leading to diminishing returns.

What Types of Systems Use Reinforcement Learning?

Reinforcement learning can be applied in many different circumstances. One of the main areas where it is used is with robotics. Machine learning systems can also be trained using reinforcement learning, and one of the main areas where it's used is in training machine learning systems to play games.

Is Reinforcement Learning Unsupervised Learning?

The answer is that reinforcement learning is not unsupervised learning. In unsupervised learning, the system is trying to find hidden patterns in a data set. In contrast, with reinforcement learning, there is a software agent, and we are trying to shape the software agent by rewarding it or punishing it when it exhibits certain behaviors while learning a skill. So, this is actually a completely different learning method as compared to unsupervised learning. The agent will use exploration strategies in order to learn and master a given skill.

Chapter 13: Regression Methods

Regression is a method that is used to predict the output value when it is numerical and continuous. As such, regression methods are particularly useful when it comes to a supervised learning problem. For example, given a set of characteristics of a patient, we might use a regression algorithm to predict their fasting blood sugar level. The inputs might include their age, race, height, weight, blood pressure, or any other measured value that might characterize the overall health of the patient and general tendencies. Another example that might be amenable to a regression type algorithm could be using age, occupation, level of education attained, zip code of home residence, city, and other data to make an estimate of their annual household income. Regression is a basic mathematical problem. It is used to fit data to a curve, so it is attempting to derive a relationship of the form $y = f(x)$ that is unknown prior to analysis.

A regression problem may have multiple variables that can be fit to a curve, as the examples above illustrate. Care must be used with regression modeling because they are particularly susceptible to overfitting and underfitting. Remember that if you overcomplicate a problem, this can lead to overfitting. There might be a lot of collected data that is not related to the problem at hand, but if you include it, the computer system will attempt to find a relationship between the irrelevant data and the output.

When real world data is then presented to the system, it will make erroneous predictions because the relationships it builds from the irrelevant data fields don't always hold. And let's also remind ourselves that if the model is too simple, it will probably miss the actual relationships that are present in the data. In this case, it is going to underfit the data, and it will probably have a large error even with the training data set.

Types of Regression

The most common type of regression that is used in machine learning is linear regression. Specifically, simple linear regression is used. This is a simple mathematical relationship between inputs and outputs. It could take a form like this:

$$Y = a + bX$$

Here, X is an input vector that consists of one or more fields or vector elements, and Y is the corresponding output vector. Y may be a single parameter. The point of this model is to use the input vector to predict the value of Y. The training process is used to determine the values of the parameters a and b. In short, you are trying to fit a straight line to a cluster of data.

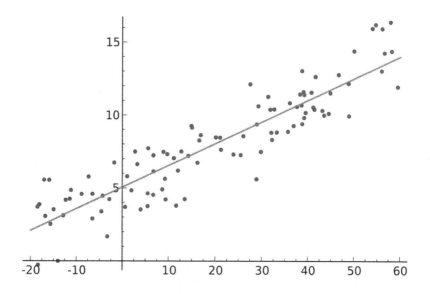

The goal of training is to determine the coefficients used to fit the training data as accurately as possible. There is always going to be some degree of error no matter how good your model is. Error can be calculated by simply taking the average squared distance between the predicted values and the measured values. Using a technique called gradient descent, the process begins by using randomly chosen parameters, and then as the data is analyzed the model updates the values of the parameters in order to minimize the error.

The size of the data set is going to be related to the level of accuracy that is achieved. Here, we are not talking about the number of fields used, which is what the dimensionality problem is about. Rather, we are simply noting that collecting more data is going to help us build a more accurate model, as long as the data is good data.

For example, if you were attempting to build a model that was predicting household income based on a given set of data fields, as you can imagine, the computer system would get more accurate if we had 1,000 data points rather than 100 data points, or if we had 10,000 data points versus 1,000 data points.

Also, the more data you have the more specific you can get in our analysis. When you only have 100 data points, the error margin is going to be so large that you really can't say anything with much confidence. But if you have thousands of data points, each data point being a person with information that may be related to the salary they make, then you can glean a large amount of relevant statistical information while also possibly drilling down more deeply.

Rather than just asking how household income is related to a number of years in school, you might also be able to ask if dog owners have a higher median income than non-dog owners.

When there are multiple input features, a more complicated relationship must be used. In this case, there are going to be multiple parameters used to fit the line. The general form is still going to be:

$$Y = a + bX$$

But this time, b is going to be an array of values, with one parameter for each feature in the input vector. If we have 6 features in the input vector, then it would be of the form:

$$Y = a + b[1]*x[1] + b[2]*x[2] ++ b[3]*x[3] + b[4]*x[4] + b[5]*x[5] + b[6]*x[6]$$

Mglearn

Mglearn is a set of helper functions that can be used in python to practice machine learning. It can be downloaded at this link:

https://github.com/amueller/introduction_to_ml_with_python

Installation instructions can be found here:

https://github.com/amueller/mglearn/blob/master/Readme.md

When using mglearn in python, you will need the following import statement:

```
import mglearn
```

You will also want to use basic plotting tools. You can include the following to generate the scatter plots that can represent test data sets:

```
import matplotlib.pylot as plt
import matplotlib
```

Since this is a tool that is designed to learn how to do machine learning, you can use it to generate datasets. To generate a dataset for the purpose of testing and learning, we can write:

```
X,y = mglearn.datasets.make_forge()
```

This will create a testing dataset that has an input vector X that can have multiple features together with labeled outputs y.

A good way to simulate the kind of data that you would encounter when faced with a linear regression problem is to make a wave of discrete points. This can be done using the make_wave command. We can label the input vector as the feature, and the output as the response. Then, you can setup an example with the number of samples that you want using the following code. Suppose that we wanted 50 samples:

```
X,y = prctlearn.datasets.make_wave(n_samples= 50)
plt.plot(X,y,'o')
plt.ylim (-4,4),
plt.xlabel("Feature")
plt.ylabel("Response")
```

This will give us something like this:

Another way to make a plot is to use linear_regression_wave. Sticking to one feature for simplicity. For example:

```
mglearn.plots.plot_linear_regression_wave()
```

The system will learn the values of the fitting parameters from the training data. This gives us:

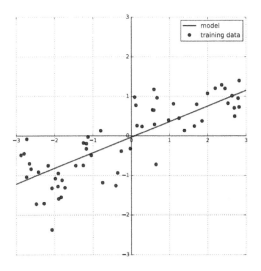

Ordinary Least Squares

Earlier we mentioned that one of the goals of our analysis is to minimize the error between the predicted values and the actual, measured values. One way that this can be done is by using what is known as the least squares method. This is what was described earlier. That is, we want to minimize the sum of the squares of the errors at each point–the error being the difference between the measured data and the value predicted by the model.

Typically, least squares is a technique that is used when a system is "overdetermined". This means that there are more equations in the system than there are unknown variables.

It is useful for linear regression because the least squares will minimize the sum of the squares of the residuals. In the case of machine learning, this means that we are going to be able to build a model of the system that is able to minimize the errors.

Logistic Regression

In many problems, the result that we want to predict is not a continuous variable, but rather a yes or no answer. For example, we might have a set of medical patients with a large amount of data collected on every patient. We might know their age, their weight, their body mass index, fasting blood sugar, systolic and diastolic blood pressure, total cholesterol, and so on. We might want to use the data collected on a patient to predict whether or not they are going to be diabetic within five years. This would enable the patient's doctor to help the patient take steps now in order to avoid becoming diabetic at some point in the future.

In order to have the system learn how to make this prediction, we would have to feed it a large training data set on past patients. This data would be labeled data, but the answer would be binary. So, we would have a large number of features on the input vector, which would be the types of medical data that we just described. The answer would be represented in binary form, with 1 = yes, the patient became diabetic within five years, or 0 = no, the patient did not become diabetic.

So, although we have a yes or no answer to the problem, this is still a regression problem.
When the answer is a binary value, we call this logistic regression. Like linear regression, the goal is to fit the data using a set of parameters from the features of the input vectors.

This type of model can be built around a threshold value. In fact, a system to detect spam email can be constructed using logistic regression.

268

So, although the end result is the email is spam (1) or it is not spam (0), in reality there is a threshold of characteristics that will determine the end result. So, you might say that it is showing 51% of the characteristics of spam, and so then it is labeled spam. The same thing would happen in our model of diabetic patients, each patient could be assigned a score, with a certain cutoff point that would reasonably predict that the patient was going to develop diabetes. And of course, we recognize that this is a reasonable approach to use because in the real world there is never going to be any certainty that a given patient can be predicted to become diabetic, although in some cases the probability might be very high.

So logistic regression can also be understood as being a kind of classification problem. Linear regression cannot be used for classification, but we can use logistic regression. Once again, this is going to be a simple linear mapping function, and so it will have the form as a linear equation:

$$Y = WX + B$$

Threshold Functions

In order to arrive at a binary result, we need to use a threshold function. There are several choices that could be used, but the most common function that is used is called the sigmoid function. Basically, the sigmoid function is 1 if x is greater than 0, and it is 0 otherwise. The graph of a sigmoid function is shown below:

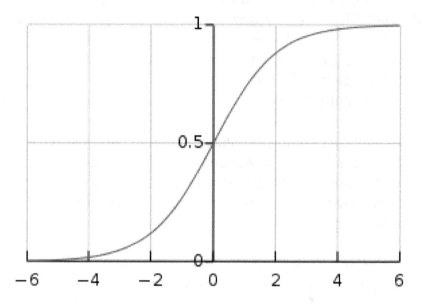

The sigmoid function can be shifted along the x axis, and so if we are calculating a probability that someone is going to be diabetic, we can set a threshold and then output a yes or no answer depending on whether or not the threshold is reached, by multiplying any result by the shifted sigmoid function. So, we could shift the origin of the sigmoid function to say 0.7, if we felt that we would want a 70% probability that a patient is going to become diabetic within five years to determine a yes answer. The details of this don't concern us here, you can simply follow the instructions of whatever tools that you are using to implement the shifted sigmoid function that you need for your purposes.

As you can see from the graph, the sigmoid function also gradually slopes down to zero. By making further adjustments, you can construct threshold functions that have a sharper boundary.

Binary and Multinomial Logistic Regression

We have already discussed the basic point of binary logistic regression. In that case there are only two possible outcomes. Of course, not every situation is that simple. If there are three or more possible ways that we can classify something, then you can use multinomial logistic regression. Suppose that we developed a machine learning system that could examine a photograph of a skin tumor and determine the type. There would actually be four different possibilities in this case.

First of all, the lesion in the photograph might be benign. It could be a plain mole that is not cancerous. Alternatively, it might be a basal cell carcinoma. It could also be a squamous cell carcinoma, and finally it might be a melanoma. Based on different values that could be calculated by the model, it would place each image that it evaluated in one of the four bins. We say that there is no order here. Of course, the doctor and patient would have their preferences, but mathematically speaking there is not any order.

If there is a problem with ordering, then we use what is known as ordinal logistic regression. In this case, the ordering of the outcomes matter, but we are still going to be sorting the data into different bins, based on the cutoff points that are assigned and the result of the regression analysis.

Chapter 14: Classification Methods

In this chapter we are going to examine some of the classification methods that are used with unsupervised learning. These are going to include things like clustering and anomaly detection. There is a little bit of overlap, in that neural networks can be used for supervised or unsupervised learning. If you are wondering why that would be–think to yourself about what a neural network is. In short, a neural network is just a brain. It is a generalized intelligent entity that can learn anything. So that should tell you that it is not a surprise that a neural network could be used to solve a problem where different types of learning are involved.

Data Transformation

Data transformation is a process of using unsupervised learning to simplify a data set. One of the most common examples of data transformation is dimensionality reduction. When data is gathered for a given problem, it may be the case that the data contains frivolous or duplicate features. Of course, if a human being is looking at the data, then it becomes a judgment call and that is something that could turn out to be wrong. However, you could take an approach of letting the machine find all the patterns in a data set, and have it throw out the features that are not predictive. Data can also be consolidated together.

Sometimes multiple features of an object can be combined together in order to arrive at a simpler representation of the data.

Clustering

Data in most situations can be clustered. If you go to a restaurant that is busy and filled with a couple of hundred people, there are many different ways that they could be sorted out. For example, you would sort everyone by age, in five year intervals, creating many clusters. Or you could divide people by gender. Or you could ask everyone their salary and then divide up people by their income. That is all clustering involves, it takes a data set and then divides up the members of the data set into different groups. When using clustering, a distance function is used to determine who is similar to whom. The idea of a distance function is based on the calculation of actual physical distance in mathematics. That is, it will have the same mathematical form, but it will use some measure of distance that is related to the problem at hand.

For example, in a given color image, each pixel is going to have a specific color value. We could start examining the data by picking out a pixel, and then building a cluster by defining a level of distance that we want to use as a threshold to say another pixel is the same color as the first one, and then group all of them together. After we have passed through all the data and pulled out all the pixels that are the first color, we do another pass and build the next cluster based on the color of the next pixel that we find.

As you can see in clustering, there is no labeling involved. The system goes through the data itself and arranges the data points into the groups that it finds, but nothing has been labeled. It is important to recognize that there are not any hard rules when it comes to clustering. In other words, the application and those involved will determine what to use to cluster the data and what the distance criteria are going to be.

Partitioning

Partitioning is a way to do clustering in machine learning. In this case, the data points are partitioned into k clusters. A distance function is used for partitioning. An example of this is k-means clustering.

Grid Methods

When using a grid method, the data space is divided up into grids. The grid like structure will consist of a large number of cells. Then clustering operations are done on the individual cells in the grid.

DBSCAN

This is a density-based clustering method. In this case, the space that the data is in is checked for density, and high-density regions are taken to have similarity as opposed to low density regions. For example, if we had a database of people from a city, we might form clusters based on age.

Those with a similar age would be assumed to be similar in other ways.

Applications

Clustering methods can be used to classify data and divide it up in many applications. One of the most popular ways that this is used in the business world is to create market segments. These are clusters of people that are assumed to have similar tastes and so forth that would be related to marketing. For example, you could form a cluster of Hispanic women aged 18-25 living in the southeast United States. Clustering is used in many scientific applications of machine learning. For example, biologists often use clustering techniques for the classification of living organisms. Earthquake zones are determined by using clustering methods. Areas that are ripe for oil and natural gas exploration can also be determined using clustering methods. In fields like insurance, clustering can be used to spot anomalous behavior, which can indicate identity theft or the filing of fraudulent claims.

K-Nearest Neighbor

The k-nearest neighbor algorithm is one that is often used for classification purposes. This process uses a "voting" method by looking at the k-nearest neighbors to a given data point. The basic idea of this algorithm is that similar objects are going to exist in proximity to one another.

Like clustering, it will use a distance function in order to determine whether or not a given data point is close enough to another object in order for us to say that they can be classified as being the same. Simple Euclidean distance is used with the k-nearest neighbor algorithm most of the time.

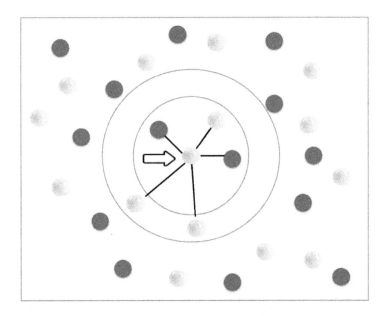

K is a value that tells the system how many neighbors to examine as a part of the algorithm. You pick an object in the data set, and then calculate the distances of the other objects from it. Then you sort the objects based on distance from smallest to largest, and then take the top K of them. The objects in the data set used here will have some labels.

So, for the K elements that have been selected you gather the labels. In a classification problem, you get the mode of the labels. For those who don't remember, a mode is the most frequently occurring data value.

So if we were doing classification by color, and our k nearest neighbors were (orange, yellow, green, orange, orange, blue, orange, green, orange), the mode would be orange. Since the nearest neighbors are orange, we choose this as our classification. The k-nearest neighbor algorithm can also be used on a regression problem. In that case, to find the value, you compute the average of the k labels.

Random Forest

A random forest is related to decision trees. In the case of a random forest, multiple decision trees are constructed during the training process. Then classification is used by having the decision trees output values, and the mode of the values returned by the decision trees is used.

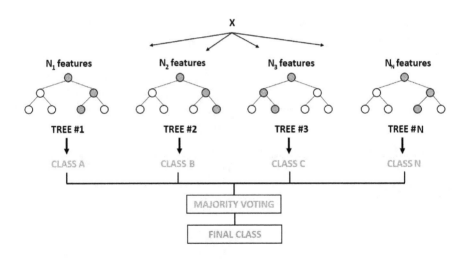

Chapter 15: TensorFlow

Tensor flow is a library built for machine learning that can be used in python. It also serves as a backend for Keras, a deep learning neural network library that we will discuss in the next chapter. The goal of TensorFlow is to make the implementation of machine learning easier. It was created by Google, and it is free to use as it is an open source library. The front-end API for TensorFlow is written in python, so you can easily use TensorFlow with programs coded using python.

Neural Networks and TensorFlow

TensorFlow is designed to work with a special type of machine learning, that is implemented using neural networks. In TensorFlow, you create graphs and data flows through the graphs. This is not anything new, the graphs that are described in TensorFlow are nodes, the same kind of nodes that are used in neural network models.

In TensorFlow, a node that is in the model is going to be a snippet of code that will implement a mathematical operation on the inputs. Then it will produce an output, that is then multiplied by a threshold function (see the following chapter) that will either let the output pass to the next layer in the network, or it will stop it from continuing forward.

Connections in TensorFlow are represented by multidimensional arrays. In mathematics, these multidimensional data arrays are called tensors.

The API is a Front End

TensorFlow helps you build fast neural network models because the interface to python is nothing more than a front end that makes using the library easy and user friendly. Rather than being interpreted like python, the TensorFlow library is compiled C++ code, and so you are actually utilizing a compiled binary file when you use TensorFlow in your models. Python is merely used as an interface to transfer data back and forth and tell the TensorFlow library to execute various operations.

Multiple Ways to Access Computing Power

One of the most powerful features of TensorFlow is that you can use different computing targets to actually perform the calculations. It is possible to use your local machine, but you can also use a cluster of computers in the cloud, and you can even utilize mobile devices to run your codes. Once you create a full working model using tensor flow, it can be deployed to any computational device. This can include a desktop computer, the cloud, or mobile devices.

TensorFlow Puts You a Step Away

The main benefit of using TensorFlow is that it does all the dirty work for you. So you don't have to sit down and actually code the tools that are used to build neural networks and do computations. Instead, these tools have already been built for you and therefore all you have to do is access them.

For readers that have used tools like Mathematica or Matlab, think of it like that. You could sit down and write your own python program to compute triple integrals, or you could just set one up in Mathematica and let it calculate it for you.

The same principle is at work here. TensorFlow is created so that you don't have to reinvent the wheel, and instead you can just use the tools that are used over and over again in the construction of neural networks. Then, when the technology changes behind the scenes, suppose that some brilliant computer scientist comes up with a better way to make neural networks, you don't have to worry about that. The people that run TensorFlow will fix things up for you behind the scenes, and you can just focus on using the library. This is a standard "black box" model of computing. You are using the black box, passing data back and forth to it, and you don't have to worry about what is inside the black box.

TensorFlow and Keras

Since TensorFlow is used in conjunction with a library called Keras, we are not going to go into the details of TensorFlow. It provides the raw power behind Keras, which is a tool that makes working with neural networks super easy. In the next chapter, we will show how to use Keras and setup tensor flow as the backend. In fact, if you look at the examples on the TensorFlow website, they are using Keras to do many of the tasks.

Chapter 16: The Keras Library

The Keras library is a python library that can be used for deep learning. Remember that deep learning is based on neural networks, which are designed to simulate the workings of the human brain in order to build systems that are capable of learning how to solve various problems and that operate autonomously. The Keras library allows you to build stand-alone models, that can be used in a "plug and play" fashion. So, you can design a model and then use it within some other context as a node that you plug in. Keras can run on top of TensorFlow.

Types of Neural Networks Used with Keras

Keras is used to create neural network building blocks. It uses standard neural networks, but Keras can also use convolutional neural networks and recurrent neural networks. The main purpose of Keras is to use python to do deep learning.

Installing Keras

In order to install Keras you must have python and the SciPy library. Keras also requires either TensorFlow or Theano. It is not necessary to install both, but at least one must be installed. Keras can run on top of either TensorFlow or Theano but can't run by itself.

You can install Keras at the command line using the following command:

sudo pip install Keras

If you have installed Keras and need to upgrade it, this can be done using the following command:

sudo pip install–upgrade Keras

This will create a configuration file for Keras in addition to installing it. The configuration file will be found in your home directory. If you open the file, you will find an entry called backend that can be used to specify whether or not it runs on TensorFlow or Theano. Alternatively, you can run this command at the command line and it will tell you to want the setting is.

You can change it if needed:

python -c "from Keras import backend; print(backend.backend())"

If you want to force it to use a different backend, then you can specify it at the command line. This example shows how to tell it to use TensorFlow and then print to confirm:

KERAS_BACKEND=TensorFlow python -c "from Keras import backend; print(backend.backend())

Creating a Deep Learning Model

A model in Keras is called a sequence. In short, this will be a stack of layers used to build a deep learning neural network. You start by creating a sequence and then adding the layers you want to add to the sequence. Next, you will specify loss functions and optimizers.

Once the setup is completed, you can train your model. Using data that you have selected as training data, you can then execute the model. The model can then be tested after training is completed. This will be done using a test data set where you know the answers. You can run the Keras model on the test data set and then compare the predictions it makes to the actual correct answers.

In order to use Keras, you will need to use numpy (see the last chapter). The backend used by Keras does not need to be specified in your python programs. So you will set up some import statements to use the library:

```
from numpy import loadtxt
from Keras.models import Sequential
from Keras.layers import Dense
```

The first step when creating a model using Keras is to load a dataset. You can use comma separated value files to import your data. Let's suppose that we are doing a classification problem, and we have a set of data in a file called testdata.csv. Assume that the data is divided into a feature vector X that has 10 features, and an output y.

The steps to load the data are:

```
# we have a comma delimited file
Mytestdata = loadtxt('testdata.csv',delimiter=',')

#extract the input features X and the output variables y
X = Mytestdata[:,0:10]
y = Mytestdata[:,10]
```

Sequential Models in Keras

Keras uses sequential models, which are deep learning models with a sequence of layers. We will create an input layer that is going to have the correct number of inputs. For each layer, we will specify the number of neurons in the layer. Some people refer to the "neurons" in a neural network as nodes. We need to determine the number of nodes in each layer. The output layer is going to have a single note, and we need to determine an activation function to use with the node.

If you recall from our discussion on neurons in a real human brain, they have a threshold that determines whether or not the neuron is going to fire and produce an output. The threshold in a human neuron is going to be determined by the electrostatic voltage. To mimic this in a neural network, we need some kind of threshold function, that will either allow information to pass or not pass. A sigmoid function is typically used.

This is a function that looks like this:

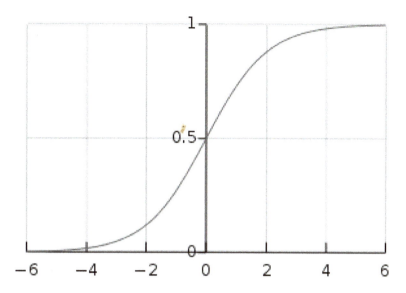

You can multiply the output by the sigmoid function, and you can see if it has not passed the threshold value (the origin in this case) the output is not passed on. We can also use a rectified linear activation function or "relu". This is sometimes called a ramp function.

The details of how it's constructed are not important for our purposes, but you should have an idea of what it looks like to get some understanding of how things are working behind the scenes:

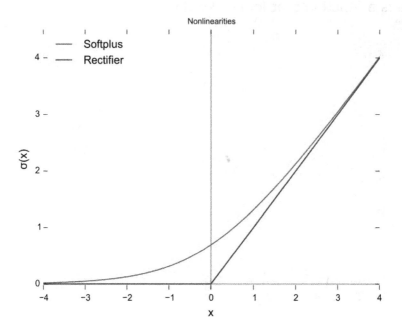

Now let's define our Keras model. At each layer, we are going to define the number of neurons to add. In the first layer the dimensions of the input are specified, and then you need to have one output layer with a single code at the end. We will have two layers in the middle. These are called hidden layers.

Remember that we have 10 inputs.

Neural_model = Sequential() # initialize the model

Now add the first layer, specifying the number of nodes, the number of inputs, and the activation function

Neural_model.add(Dense(16, input_dim=10, activation = 'relu'))

```
#Add two hidden layers
Neural_model.add( Dense(8,activation = 'relu'))
Neural_model.add( Dense(8,activation = 'relu'))

#Finally, add the output node
Neural_model.add( Dense(1,activation = 'sigmoid'))
```

Once you have specified the construction of the model, you can compile it, using the compile command. When you compile your model, you will have to specify a few parameters. These are the loss function, the optimizing function, and metrics. A neural network needs to use weights to determine the strength of connections between different nodes, so the optimizer that is specified tells it how to determine the weights.

Suppose that for our example we have a binary classification problem, which is actually quite common for neural networks. The loss function in that case that you want to pass to Keras is binary_crossentropy. Adam is an optimizer for weights that uses gradient descent. Finally, we use accuracy for the metric when doing binary classification. The full setup, specified when executing the compile command in your python program, is as follows:

```
Neural_model.compile( loss = 'binary_crossentropy', optimizer = 'adam',
metrics = ['accuracy')
```

Training the Model

After the model has been defined and compiled, then you will train it on some data. This is done using the 'fit' command, which will attempt to fit the training data that you expose to the model. In Keras, training is done using epochs. An epoch is a single pass through all the rows in the training data set. You are going to specify multiple epochs, which simply means that it will pass through the data multiple times. As the model passes through the data, at some point as it's being exposed to the data it may want to update the weights inside the model. You use a batch size to tell it how many data samples to pass through before it updates the weights. This is done by setting the batch size.

So, an epoch is really nothing more than an iteration where the model revisits the data with multiple passes. By exposing it to the data many times, you can make the model better. Think of it as studying, if you read a chapter you are going to be tested on once, you might not do so well. If you read chapter 3 times and study it, then you are likely to pass the exam. The same principle sort of applies here, each time that the model goes through the data, the weights will be adjusted, making the model better.

Of course, at some point we are going to get into a situation of diminishing returns, in other words continuing to pass over the data no longer causes significant updates to the weights. You have to use judgment, based on experience, to know what works. If you expose the model to testing data after this process and it is not very accurate, then you might conclude that you didn't use enough epochs to train the data, or your batch size was not appropriately chosen.

In any case, you can train the model with a single line in your python program:

```
Neural_model.fit(X, y, epochs = 200, batch_size = 10)
```

When you are working with deep learning neural networks, the error is going to settle down to some value. There is always going to be a degree of error, it is not possible to create an error free system.

However, when it settles down to the minimal error that is possible given the data and the setup that you have created, this is known as convergence.

Testing a Keras Model

The next step after training is to test the model. This is done using the evaluate command, and you can get an estimate of the accuracy of the model at this point to determine if the model is where you want it to be. In order to evaluate a Keras model, you can use a new testing data set in the same way that you would with any other machine learning program. Again, this is going to be a one-step command, but first we have to load our test data. When you evaluate a model, it will return a single float value, the accuracy.

```
#Load Test Data
Test_data = loadtxt('test_data.csv', delimiter = ',')
X_t = Test_data[:,0:10]
y_t = Test_data[:,10]

result = Neural_model.evaluate(X_t,y_t)
print('Accuracy is : %.2f' %(accuracy * 100))
```

Making Predictions with a Keras Model

Finally, you can use a Keras model that has been trained to make predictions. You will do this assuming that the model has attained an acceptable level of accuracy. This is done by passing it an input data set, but no output values (after all, it is a prediction and you don't know what the output values are). Predictions can be returned in pairs so that you can see the prediction y for every input X. Assume that X_i is some new input data that we have loaded into the system from a csv file of input data. Assume also that we have 100 elements.

```
Predictions = Neural_model.predict(X_i)
For i in range(100):
  Print(predictions[i],y[i])
```

Summary

As you can see, if you want to build deep learning neural networks, Keras makes it pretty simple. Of course, doing it the right way is something that you are going to have to work towards by gaining more experience as time goes on.
The nice thing about Keras is that it makes it very easy to build, train, and test neural networks and then get the information that you need out of them. And even better it's free to use.

Chapter 17: The Scikit-Learn Library

In this chapter we are going to introduce the Scikit-learn library. This is a set of tools for python that are used for the purposes of data mining and data analysis. These tools are reusable and the library is able to perform many of the common tasks used in machine learning. For example, it can do regression, classification, dimensionality reduction, clustering, and preprocessing.

Background: What is Data Mining?

In short, data mining is examining large data sets in order to extract the patterns, anomalies, and correlations that are hidden in the data. Data mining has been used in the business world for a long period of time, and although it is a task that is well suited for machine learning, it's not specifically associated with machine learning. That said, for our purposes we will want to look at it from a machine learning perspective. There are several ways that data mining is used in business. For example, an analysis of large data sets can help a company cut its costs, or it can be used to help provide better customer service. The range of applications for data mining is large, any task that you can think of for a business that is important is something that can be solved with data mining provided that the large data sets that are required exist and are accessible.

Data mining simply refers to going through large data sets in order to find the patterns in the data that can describe useful relationships or make predictions. In short, this is nothing new. Different types of modeling are used in data mining. These include descriptive modeling, predictive modeling, and prescriptive modeling. Descriptive modeling involves discovering shared similarities or clustering in historical data. Clustering is used to group similar data points or records together. Descriptive modeling can also be used to identify anomalies, by finding outliers that don't fit into any of the clusters that can be built in a large data set. Descriptive modeling is also used to find previously hidden relationships that might exist between members of a data set.

In predictive modeling, we move from an analysis of historical data to use past data in order to predict future results. When we move into predictive modeling, we are encountering many of the familiar methods that are used in machine learning. Tools used in predictive modeling include neural networks, regression models, decision trees, and support vector machines. Finally, prescriptive modeling seeks to utilize unstructured data in predictive models.

The Data Mining Process

Data mining goes through a series of steps designed to select, modify, and gather the information that may be contained in large data sets. The first step is selection of the data to be used. Then it will go through a process of preprocessing in order to prepare it for the data mining process. This may include assembling data from many different sources or data warehouses, and assembling it into a new and unified form that is suitable for the analysis. Dimensionality reduction and other techniques may also be used in order to make the data more suitable for machine learning methods. Then, the various methods used for data mining are applied to the data set.

Datasets in Scikit-Learn

Scikit learn has several data sets that can be used for the purposes of practice. These are available in the dataset loading utilities. They are referred to as toy datasets. The data sets that are currently available include:

- *Boston*: This includes a dataset of Boston house prices that is suitable for regression problems. It includes a large number of fields that may or may not be relevant for something you are analyzing. For example, it includes the per capita crime rate and a median value of homes in the area, but also includes the concentration of nitrous oxides in the neighborhood.
- *Iris*: The iris data set contains information about iris flowers. The purpose of this dataset is to learn about using classification methods.
- *Diabetes*: The diabetes dataset includes ten features that may be relevant to diabetes, including age, sex, body mass index and other parameters. The dataset includes data on 442 patients. This is another regression dataset.
- *Digits*: the purpose of this dataset is to study optical recognition using handwritten digits. It has 64 features and 5620 elements. This is to study classification.
- *Linnerrud*: this is a dataset that can be used to study multivariate regression. It is a small dataset with only 20 instances, with 3 features, but there are two sets, physiological features that measure weight, waist circumference, and pulse, with the other set containing exercise performance results.
- *Breast Cancer*: this is another classification data set. It includes 569 members, each with 30 features that describe a breast cancer tumor.

Several real-world datasets are also available on the site. To load a data set, you first need to import sklearn and the appropriate libraries into your python code. It is also necessary to import numpy. For this example, consider using the diabetes dataset.

The necessary import statements are:

```
import matplotlib.pyplot as plt
import numpy as np
from sklearn import datasets, linear_model
from sklearn.metrics import mean_squared_error, r2_score
```

Next, we need to load the data set:

```
diabetes = datasets.load_diabetes()
```

Splitting Data into Training and Testing

The next step is to select data that will be used for training the machine learning system, and then for testing it. The first step in scikit is to specify what features are used. In this example, we can pick a feature to use:

```
diabetes_X = diabetes.data[:, np.newaxis, 2]
```

Now you can split the data into subsets, one for training and one for testing. This needs to be done for inputs X and outputs y.

```
diabetes_X_train = diabetes_X[:-20]
diabetes_X_test = diabetes_X[-20:]

diabetes_y_train = diabetes.target[:-20]
diabetes_y_test = diabetes.target[-20:]
```

Doing Linear Regression and Training

Using scikit, doing linear regression and testing is extremely simple. Everything that you need for doing our analysis is already built for you, you simply need the data to run it on. For the example given here, we use a linear regression model in order to build a predictive model based on the features used in the analysis. Training the model is done with one line of code.

```
regr = linear_model.LinearRegression()
regr.fit(diabetes_X_train, diabetes_y_train)
```

Now that the model has been trained, we can test the model by having it make predictions, and then comparing that to the known results. A variance of 1 would be a perfect prediction, so the distance between the reported result and unity will tell us how good the model is.

```
diabetes_y_pred = regr.predict(diabetes_X_test)
print('Coefficients: \n', regr.coef_)
print("Mean squared error: %.2f"
      % mean_squared_error(diabetes_y_test,
diabetes_y_pred))
print('Variance score: %.2f' %
r2_score(diabetes_y_test, diabetes_y_pred))
```

Here we plot the output:

```
plt.scatter(diabetes_X_test, diabetes_y_test,
color='black')
plt.plot(diabetes_X_test, diabetes_y_pred,
color='blue', linewidth=3)

plt.xticks(())
plt.yticks(())

plt.show()
```

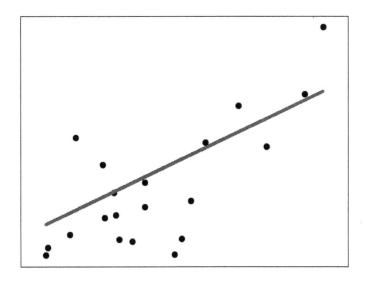

Using SciKit for Solving Other Types of Problems

Many of the toy and real-world datasets provided with Scikit can be used to do classification problems, clustering analysis, anomaly detection, and more. In this example found on the scikit-learn.org website, we see how to use outlier detection. The data used for this example is the Boston dataset with housing data. Covariance methods are considering two different relationships. In the first case, an anomaly is found considering the pupil-teacher relationship versus the accessibility to highways. In the second example, we look for anomalies in a dataset that is distributed quite differently, considering the average number of rooms per household against the % lower status of the population. This will show you how to use classifiers in order to detect outlying or anomalous data. We begin by importing the needed libraries. As always you will need to import numpy, and the plotting and dataset libraries. You will also need to import the covariance library.

The example code here was created by Virgile Fritsch.

```
import numpy as np
from sklearn.covariance import EllipticEnvelope
from sklearn.svm import OneClassSVM
import matplotlib.pyplot as plt
import matplotlib.font_manager
from sklearn.datasets import load_boston
```

We begin by loading the data. It is helpful to look at plots of the data now, so that we can understand what the programmer is referring to. First, you see the two-cluster data, with a significant outlier. Below, we see the banana shaped data.

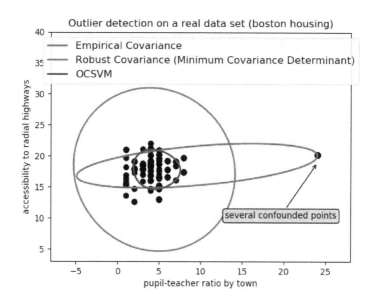

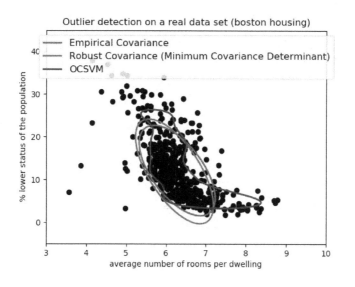

Here is the code that is used to load the data. The values used indicate the particular features and outputs that we want to use in each data set.

```
X1 = load_boston()['data'][:, [8, 10]]  # two clusters
X2 = load_boston()['data'][:, [5, 12]]  # "banana"-shaped
```

Next, the classifiers are defined.

```
classifiers = {
    "Empirical Covariance": EllipticEnvelope(support_fraction=1.,
                        contamination=0.261),
    "Robust Covariance (Minimum Covariance Determinant)":
    EllipticEnvelope(contamination=0.261),
    "OCSVM": OneClassSVM(nu=0.261, gamma=0.05)}
colors = ['m', 'g', 'b']
legend1 = {}
legend2 = {}
```

In order to detect outliers, you need to have the computer learn where the 'frontier' is so that it can then detect outliers.

This is accomplished with the following statements:

```python
xx1, yy1 = np.meshgrid(np.linspace(-8, 28, 500), np.linspace(3, 40, 500))
xx2, yy2 = np.meshgrid(np.linspace(3, 10, 500), np.linspace(-5, 45, 500))
for i, (clf_name, clf) in enumerate(classifiers.items()):
    plt.figure(1)
    clf.fit(X1)
    Z1 = clf.decision_function(np.c_[xx1.ravel(), yy1.ravel()])
    Z1 = Z1.reshape(xx1.shape)
    legend1[clf_name] = plt.contour(
        xx1, yy1, Z1, levels=[0], linewidths=2, colors=colors[i])
    plt.figure(2)
    clf.fit(X2)
    Z2 = clf.decision_function(np.c_[xx2.ravel(), yy2.ravel()])
    Z2 = Z2.reshape(xx2.shape)
    legend2[clf_name] = plt.contour(
        xx2, yy2, Z2, levels=[0], linewidths=2, colors=colors[i])

legend1_values_list = list(legend1.values())
legend1_keys_list = list(legend1.keys())
```

Now we can plot the data. First, we plot the two-cluster data:

```
plt.figure(1)  # two clusters
plt.title("Outlier detection on a real data set (boston housing)")
plt.scatter(X1[:, 0], X1[:, 1], color='black')
bbox_args = dict(boxstyle="round", fc="0.8")
arrow_args = dict(arrowstyle="->")
plt.annotate("several confounded points", xy=(24, 19),
        xycoords="data", textcoords="data",
        xytext=(13, 10), bbox=bbox_args, arrowprops=arrow_args)
plt.xlim((xx1.min(), xx1.max()))
plt.ylim((yy1.min(), yy1.max()))
plt.legend((legend1_values_list[0].collections[0],
        legend1_values_list[1].collections[0],
        legend1_values_list[2].collections[0]),
        (legend1_keys_list[0], legend1_keys_list[1], legend1_keys_list[2]),
        loc="upper center",
        prop=matplotlib.font_manager.FontProperties(size=12))
plt.ylabel("accessibility to radial highways")
plt.xlabel("pupil-teacher ratio by town")

legend2_values_list = list(legend2.values())
legend2_keys_list = list(legend2.keys())
```

Then plot the banana shaped data:

```
plt.figure(2)  # "banana" shape
plt.title("Outlier detection on a real data set (boston housing)")
plt.scatter(X2[:, 0], X2[:, 1], color='black')
plt.xlim((xx2.min(), xx2.max()))
plt.ylim((yy2.min(), yy2.max()))
plt.legend((legend2_values_list[0].collections[0],
        legend2_values_list[1].collections[0],
        legend2_values_list[2].collections[0]),
        (legend2_keys_list[0], legend2_keys_list[1], legend2_keys_list[2]),
        loc="upper center",
        prop=matplotlib.font_manager.FontProperties(size=12))
plt.ylabel("% lower status of the population")
plt.xlabel("average number of rooms per dwelling")

plt.show()
```

The plots show that the outliers have been detected.

Summary

Scikit is a very comprehensive but easy to use tool that can be used with python for machine learning and data mining. The tool is free to use and there are many coding samples that can be downloaded to help you learn how to use this tool to do many of the common tasks that are done in machine learning. Rather than having to write many lines of code in order to implement testing and other tasks, Scikit-learn enables you to use its built-in functionality in order to write clean and short code snippets that can do some pretty sophisticated analysis.

Chapter 18: NumPy

NumPy is a library of scientific computing routines that are used in Python. The main purpose of NumPy is to allow you to perform many operations that are used on matrices. It will enable you to do faster calculations and build more sophisticated models, because the arrays used in NumPy go beyond what is available with standard lists in Python. NumPy is a library that you are going to need to use with many of the tools that have been described in this book. NumPy can actually be thought of as a wrapper. There is pre-compiled C code that works underneath the NumPy interface that you see as a Python programmer. The pre-compiled code enables NumPy to perform calculations with large matrices and vectors very quickly.

Ndarray

Ndarray is the most fundamental object in the NumPy library. The label simply means an N-dimensional array. Every element in a ndarray is the same data type. So, while you may be used to mixing up data types in lists with Python, you can't do that with an ndarray. An ndarray can be initialized in code using the array method and specifying the data elements that are in the array. First, you have to import the NumPy library into your python code.

This is done like this:

```
import numpy as mynumpy
```

Now, mynumpy is an object that we can refer to and use throughout our code. For example, we can create a simple vector with three elements like this:

my_vector = mynumpy.array([1.3, 4.1, 10.8])

Notice that all three elements in the array are the same data type. So, we could not type:

my_vector = mynumby.array([1.3, 'sam',10.8])

We could also create a matrix, by specifying the two rows in the matrix. This is an example of a 2x2 matrix:

import numpy as mynumpy

2d_matrix = mynumpy.array([[1,2],[3,4]])

Now let's create a 2 x 3 matrix:

2by3 = mynumpy.array([[3,8,2],[5,2,7]])

The shape command will give the number of rows and columns in the matrix. You can also extract the number of dimensions, and the shape and size of the array, along with the data type of the elements.

These examples are illustrated with this code:

```
print("Shape of 2d: ", 2d_matrix.shape)
print("Shape of 2 by 3: ", 2by3.shape)

print("Size of the 2 by 3 ", 2by3.size)

print("Dimensions of first array: ", 2d_matrix.ndim)
```

The results are:

```
Shape of 2d: (2,2)
Shape of 2 by 3: (2,3)
Size of the 2 by 3: 6
Dimensions of first array: 2
```

To get the data type, use the dtype command:

```
print(2by3.dtype)
```

This will print int64. Arrays can be created for any numerical data type in python, such as float or complex. You can also use the zeros command to create an array (or technically a matrix) that has a specified number of rows and columns that are all initialized to zero. For example:

```
voltages = mynumpy.zeros((5,7))
```

That has created a 5 x 7 matrix filled with zeros called voltages. There is one exception to the rule that the elements of an array have to be the same data type, you can create an array of python objects using NumPy, and each object can contain data of different types. In the context of machine learning, you are going to be using arrays that contain the same type of data.

Creating a Column Vector

Creating column vectors is something that is routinely done in the context of linear algebra. To create a column vector using numpy, simply follow the syntax shown here.
In the first example we create a column vector with two elements, and in the second example we create a column vector with three elements, and then we create a row vector with three elements:

```
import numpy as my_numpy

vector_2 = my_numpy.array( [[3],[6]] )

vector_3 = my_numpy.array( [2],[7],[9] )

row_vector = my_numpy.array( [1,6,9] )
```

Size of NumPy Arrays

It is important to note that the size of a NumPy array is fixed when you first declare it. The reason that we need to mention this is that python lists can grow dynamically when the program is running, and so those who have experience with python will find that this is not the kind of behavior that they are used to.

High Level Operations on Arrays

NumPy is also used to perform high level operations on arrays, which facilitates the use of NumPy arrays in the context of advanced and complex mathematical operations.

Dot Product

In many contexts, calculating the dot product between two vectors is a common calculation that must be carried out. First let's set up two vectors and then use the dot command to print out the result. Remember that the dot product produces a scalar result.

```
import numpy as my_numpy

vector_A = my_numpy.array ( [1,4,5] )
vector_B = my_numby.array ( [2,3,5] )

print(my_numpy.dot(vector_A,vector_B)
```

Get the Eigenvalues and Eigenvectors of a Matrix

NumPy can use the linear algebra library *eig* function to return the eigenvalues and eigenvectors of a matrix simultaneously.

```
import numpy as my_numpy

#Create a Matrix
matrix = my_numpy.array([[2,2,3],[1,5,9],[11,8,8]])
print(matrix)

# Calculate the Eigenvalues and Eigenvectors of the Matrix
eigenvalues ,eigenvectors = my_numpy.linalg.eig(matrix)
print(eigenvalues)
print(eigenvectors)
```

Matrix Inversion

Another common task that is used with square matrices is to invert a matrix. Again, you will use linalg, and this illustrates how NumPy wraps complicated mathematical operations into simple one-line statements.

```
import numpy as my_numpy

Matrix = my_numpy.array ( [1,2,3], [4,5,6], [7,8,9] )
Print(Matrix)

#invert the matrix
Inverted_Matrix = my_numpy.linalg.inv(Matrix)
Print(Inverted_Matrix)
```

Trace of a Matrix

In many scientific contexts. The trace of a matrix is an important piece of data. This can be found by using the trace command.

```
import numpy as my_numpy

#Create a Matrix
matrix = my_numpy.array([[1,2,3],[4,5,6],[7,8,9]])

print(matrix)

print(matrix.trace())
```

Random Number Generation

Finally, it can be useful to generate random numbers. In this case we generate four random numbers ranging over 1 and 20, and then we generate five numbers from a normal distribution with a mean of 5.2 and standard deviation of 1.3:

```
import numpy as my_numpy

my_numpy.random.seed(1)

print(my_numpy.randint(0,21,4))

print(my_numpy.random.normal(5.2,1.3,5))
```

Creating a Neural Network Using Numpy

One of the powerful features of numpy is that you can use the matrices and mathematical operations that are built into the library to create neural networks. In the following example, which is borrowed from python-course.eu, a simple network with one hidden layer is developing using numpy and python alone.

Of course, doing this without using one of the libraries that have been described in the book means that you are going to be doing a lot of coding yourself that isn't really necessary. In my view you may as well use a library that is already fully developed for this purpose. However, we will include their example here so that you can see that it is possible to build up a neural network using python alone, and you can do other tasks like linear regression.

In the example used, a neural network class is defined. Weight matrices are created to calculate the weights between the nodes that are in the neural network.

The threshold used is the sigmoid function.

The entire code is here:

```python
import numpy as np
@np.vectorize
def sigmoid(x):
    return 1 / (1 + np.e ** -x)
activation_function = sigmoid
from scipy.stats import truncnorm
def truncated_normal(mean=0, sd=1, low=0, upp=10):
    return truncnorm(
        (low - mean) / sd, (upp - mean) / sd, loc=mean, scale=sd)
class NeuralNetwork:
    def __init__(self,
                 no_of_in_nodes,
                 no_of_out_nodes,
                 no_of_hidden_nodes,
                 learning_rate,
                 bias=None
                 ):
        self.no_of_in_nodes = no_of_in_nodes
        self.no_of_out_nodes = no_of_out_nodes

        self.no_of_hidden_nodes = no_of_hidden_nodes

        self.learning_rate = learning_rate
        self.bias = bias
        self.create_weight_matrices()

    def create_weight_matrices(self):
        """ A method to initialize the weight matrices of the neural
        network with optional bias nodes"""
```

```python
        bias_node = 1 if self.bias else 0
    rad = 1 / np.sqrt(self.no_of_in_nodes + bias_node)
    X = truncated_normal(mean=0, sd=1, low=-rad, upp=rad)
    self.weights_in_hidden = X.rvs((self.no_of_hidden_nodes,
                    self.no_of_in_nodes + bias_node))
    rad = 1 / np.sqrt(self.no_of_hidden_nodes + bias_node)
    X = truncated_normal(mean=0, sd=1, low=-rad, upp=rad)
    self.weights_hidden_out = X.rvs((self.no_of_out_nodes,
                    self.no_of_hidden_nodes + bias_node))


def train(self, input_vector, target_vector):
    # input_vector and target_vector can be tuple, list or ndarray

    bias_node = 1 if self.bias else 0
    if self.bias:
        # adding bias node to the end of the inpuy_vector
        input_vector = np.concatenate( (input_vector, [self.bias]) )

    input_vector = np.array(input_vector, ndmin=2).T
    target_vector = np.array(target_vector, ndmin=2).T

    output_vector1 = np.dot(self.weights_in_hidden, input_vector)
    output_vector_hidden = activation_function(output_vector1)

    if self.bias:
        output_vector_hidden = np.concatenate(
(output_vector_hidden, [[self.bias]]) )


    output_vector2 = np.dot(self.weights_hidden_out,
output_vector_hidden)
```

```python
        output_vector_network = activation_function(output_vector2)
        output_errors = target_vector - output_vector_network
        # update the weights:
        tmp = output_errors * output_vector_network * (1.0 -
output_vector_network)
        tmp = self.learning_rate  * np.dot(tmp, output_vector_hidden.T)
        self.weights_hidden_out += tmp
        # calculate hidden errors:
        hidden_errors = np.dot(self.weights_hidden_out.T,
output_errors)
        # update the weights:
        tmp = hidden_errors * output_vector_hidden * (1.0 -
output_vector_hidden)
        if self.bias:
            x = np.dot(tmp, input_vector.T)[:-1,:]    # ???? last element cut
off, ???
        else:
            x = np.dot(tmp, input_vector.T)
        self.weights_in_hidden += self.learning_rate * x


    def run(self, input_vector):
        # input_vector can be tuple, list or ndarray

        if self.bias:
            # adding bias node to the end of the inpuy_vector
            input_vector = np.concatenate( (input_vector, [1]) )
        input_vector = np.array(input_vector, ndmin=2).T
        output_vector = np.dot(self.weights_in_hidden, input_vector)
        output_vector = activation_function(output_vector)
```

```python
if self.bias:
    output_vector = np.concatenate( (output_vector, [[1]]) )

output_vector = np.dot(self.weights_hidden_out, output_vector)
output_vector = activation_function(output_vector)

return output_vector
```

Conclusion

Thank you for making it through to the end of *Python Machine Learning*, let's hope it was informative and able to provide you with all of the tools you need to achieve your goals whatever they may be.

Machine learning is an exciting and rapidly evolving field. While mastery of the subject can involve many years of study, it is possible to get started quickly by gaining some basic familiarity with the methods and goals of machine learning. Many of the machine learning methods, despite the mysterious aura that surrounds the field, are actually relatively simple mathematical tools that have literally been around for centuries. It is just now that they are being applied to the massive amounts of data, the so-called big data, that is being collected by companies and other large organizations.

Python is an excellent tool to use for learning about–machine learning. Python is a very simple programming language that most people are able to pick up rather quickly. Libraries have been developed for python that is specifically designed for machine learning, and so it is easy for a developer to play around with the tools and actually solve simple machine learning problems.

The way to go forward is to actually practice and study more. Begin by going through any exercises that you can find that entail covering all of the major algorithms that are used in machine learning.

Using both supervised and unsupervised learning is important, as anyone who wants to understand machine learning needs to become intimately familiar with both. You should also practice by using many of the standard algorithms like linear regression and k-nearest neighbors.

Something that I would suggest is to avoid getting trapped into only using generated test data. To enhance your learning and development, get a hold of real-world data sets that you can run your algorithms on so that you can gain an even greater familiarity with the practice of data science.

Many people who are new to the concept of machine learning ask what specific educational credentials they need in order to get into the field. While there are some general guidelines, the truth is there are no specific rules. We can begin by saying that in all likelihood, anyone who is involved in a scientific or technical field of study would be in a position to get involved in machine learning. That certainly applies to electrical or computer engineers.

However, some people that might be better placed to get into machine learning are mathematicians that are experts in statistics and probability. Some crossover knowledge can be helpful, but in some ways, when it comes down to the day-to-day practice of a data scientist, the field of machine learning is really a statistical field. Certainly, a high level of knowledge of statistics and probability is helpful.

Since it is considered a crossover discipline background in computer science can be helpful. The ideal candidate would be someone who has a substantial background in computer science that has also demonstrated a high-level education in statistics. The more advanced your education, the more deeply you can go into the field, including doing AI research and designing more advanced systems.

If you are just playing around with some models, you are not going to be designing machine learning systems for use in some new robotic systems. That will require advanced education in computer science.

However, there are varying roles and levels of machine learning. Those who study computer systems in business school, provided that they have a good understanding of statistics, are going to be well-suited for doing machine learning tasks as a data scientist at many companies. Simply analyzing customer data or internal company data for trends and patterns is not something that requires a deep understanding of artificial intelligence, and your role is to use the tools of machine learning that are available in order to extract the kind of information that is useful for the enterprise.

So, machine learning and data science are fields that have a wide range of complexity and application. There is virtually some level of expertise that is going to be suitable for many different levels and types of education, background, and taste. It is definitely a growing field for the future. In this book we have learned what machine learning is, and how it is applied today by businesses to many different tasks.

We learned that there is supervised and unsupervised learning, and how they are different. We also learned the issues that might crop up with various tradeoffs in machine learning. We also learned many of the major algorithms that are used in machine learning, including regression methods, k-nearest neighbor methods, and decision trees. A large part of building a solid and reliable machine learning system is selecting the most appropriate training data sets and the best algorithm for a given situation.

This in part is going to be determined by your experience, and the more experience that you get practicing machine learning, the better you are going to be when it comes to selecting the right algorithms for a given problem.

We also saw how python could be used to implement some of the most common machine learning tasks. We used python for regressing, k-nearest neighbors, and other classification methods. We looked at the TensorFlow library, the Sciikit learn library, and the Numpy library. We also learned about Keras, and saw how to build a neural network. The power of Numpy lies behind many of the tools used to build machine learning models with python.

So where to go from here? The first step is to keep learning. You should keep practicing by building more models, and using different tools to build your models. However, there is more to machine learning than simply playing around with tools. You should read as many books as you can and watch videos from reputable sources, so that you can learn the theory and fundamentals that lie behind the concept of machine learning.

If you go further than this, it will in large part depend on your current situation and your goals for the future. If you are already a working professional, you might not need to go to school and get a degree in computer science.

You might be learning the tools described in this book for the sake of practical application at your current job. If that is the case, then practice along with self-study is the best path forward for you, although of course if you are willing and able to return to school to get an in-depth education on the subject, that is always an option.

For those that are just getting exposed to the field and looking to it in order to pick a career path, getting a college degree in computer science or a related subject is probably the best way forward for you, especially if you are hoping to attain employment. The fields of data science and machine learning are not likely to be fields where too many people are able to get employment without some kind of college degree in a related field. If possible, find a school that will let you get a concentration in artificial intelligence and machine learning. I would also advise taking many math classes that are focused on statistics and probability. Some "business acumen" is often advised, so it can't hurt to take some management classes as well. This is recommended even though many technical types are not that enthusiastic about business school. You are not going there to become an MBA, but you should get some idea of business operations at a large corporation and learn about many business concepts like business intelligence, predictive analytics, and data mining, since these are useful concepts for corporations and they prefer people that have some understanding of this to join their team, ready to hit the ground running. Computer engineering is a related field that can also be pursued, and you can even consider mechanical engineering. That might not come to mind right away, but remember that in mechanical engineering there is a lot of research in the area of robotics. But remember that college is nothing more than an entry ticket. Machine learning is a very practical field, and many of the tools described in this book are what is going to be used in the real world. I hope that this book has stimulated your interest in machine learning, and that it will help propel you to continue your education and development in this exciting area.

www.ingramcontent.com/pod-product-compliance
Lightning Source LLC
Chambersburg PA
CBHW071103050326
40690CB00008B/1101